Gallery Books
Editor: Peter Fallon

THREE SISTERS

Brian Friel

Anton Chekhov's
Three Sisters

A translation

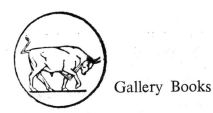

Gallery Books

Three Sisters
is first published
simultaneously in
paperback and in a
clothbound edition
on September 8, 1981.

The Gallery Press
19 Oakdown Road
Dublin 14. Ireland.

© Brian Friel 1981

Cover design by Michael Kane

ISBN   0 904011 26 7 (paper)
       904011 25 9 (cloth)

All professional and amateur rights in this play are strictly
reserved and applications to perform it must be made in advance
to Spokesmen, 1 Craven Hill, London W2 3EW.
This book is published with the help of the Arts Council (An
Chomhairle Ealaíon) and the Arts Council of Northern Ireland.
Printed in Ireland by the Leinster Leader, Naas, Co. Kildare.

for Sally and David

Field Day's production of *Three Sisters* opened in the Guildhall, Derry, on Tuesday, 8 September, 1981, with the following cast:

Olga	Sorcha Cusack
Masha	Eileen Pollock
Irina	Olwen Fouere
Andrey	John Quinn
Fyodor Kulygin	Patrick Waldron
Alexander Vershinin	James Ellis
Ivan Chebutykin	Eamon Kelly
Vassily Solyony	Colm Meaney
Baron Tusenbach	Niall Buggy
Natasha	Nuala Hayes
Vladimir Roddey	Michael Burlington
Alexey Fedotik	Gary Lilburn
Anfisa	Máirín D. O'Sullivan
Ferapont	Michael Duffy
Director	Stephen Rea
Designer	Eileen Diss
Lighting Designer	Rory Dempster
Costumes	Dany Everett
Music	Mícheál Ó Súilleabháin
Artist	Basil Blackshaw

ACT ONE

The Prozorov house is situated outside a large provincial Russian town (population 100,000) and close to a river.

It is the month of May, a bright and sunny Sunday morning just before noon.

A drawingroom with columns beyond which is a large diningroom. In the drawingroom there is a draught-screen, a large iron stove, a full-size mirror, a piano.

In both the drawingroom and the diningroom there are spring flowers everywhere—flowers on the tables, flowers on the piano, flowers on the mantlepiece, flowers in vases on the floor; a profusion of flowers, almost an excess of flowers.

ANFISA is helping and supervising two young maids who are laying the diningroom table for buffet lunch.

OLGA is wearing the regulation dark blue dress of a secondary schoolteacher. She is correcting exercise books.

MASHA is dressed in black; her hat on her lap; reading.

IRINA is in a white dress. She has a basket filled with flowers and is arranging them in vases around the room.

Silence except for the sound of ANDREY playing the violin in his room off right.

OLGA stops working. She looks first at MASHA, then at IRINA. Then she speaks. IRINA continues arranging her flowers for a few seconds and then stops to listen.

OLGA   It's hard to believe it's only a year since father's death, isn't it? Twelve months to the day. The fifth of May. Your birthday, Irina. Do you remember how cold it was? And there was snow falling. I thought then I'd never get over it. And you collapsed—d'you remember?—passed out cold. But a year *has* gone by and we can talk about it calmly now, can't we? Of course we can. And you're wearing white again and you look . . . radiant! *(Clock strikes.)* The clock struck twelve then too. Remember the band playing when they were carrying the coffin out of the room here? And firing the salute in the cemetery? General Prozorov, Brigade Commander! All the same very few local people turned up. But it was a terrible day, wasn't it? All

	that rain and snow and ——
IRINA	*(Closing her eyes)* Olga, please!

BARON TUSENBACH, DOCTOR CHEBUTYKIN *and* CAPTAIN SOLYONY *enter the diningroom and talk in undertones among themselves and to* ANFISA. CHEBUTYKIN *is engrossed in his paper.* OLGA *opens all the windows. As she does*

OLGA There's real warmth in the air today, isn't there? It's such a relief to be able to fling the windows wide open. And we won't feel until the birch trees are in leaf. I'm sure they're already in leaf in Moscow . . . D'you remember the day we left there? Eleven years ago, but I remember it as if it were yesterday. Father had finally got his brigade and we were posted here. Early in May. Just like now. And it seemed as if everything was just about to . . . to blossom. And Moscow, beautiful, beautiful Moscow was bathed in sunshine and warmth. Eleven whole years. What happened to them? But when I woke this morning and saw the heat-haze I knew that finally, finally spring had come. And I felt—I felt elated. No, exalted! And suddenly and with all my soul I longed, I yearned to go back home again.

CHEBUTYKIN *(Tapping his paper)* Rubbish-rubbish-rubbish.

BARON You're right, Doctor. All words—all rubbish.

MASHA, *absorbed in her book, whistles softly through her teeth.*

OLGA Masha, would you mind . . . please . . . my migraine's back. All day at school and all evening at this *(Corrections)*—it's turning me into a crabbed old maid, isn't it? Do you realise: I'm four years in that secondary school and every day, every single hour of every day, I can actually feel my youth and my energy draining away. All I'm left with is a resolution, a determination, a passion ——

IRINA To go back to Moscow.

OLGA Yes!

IRINA   To sell this house, to pack up here and to go home to Moscow.

OLGA   Yes! Yes! Home to Moscow! But it must be soon, Irina! It has got to be soon!

CHEBUTYKIN *and the doctor both laugh.*

IRINA   Once Andrey becomes a professor he won't stay on here. So there'll be nothing to stop us—*(Remembering)* except poor Masha.

OLGA   Masha'll come and spend the summer in Moscow—the whole summer, every summer!

MASHA *whistles softly.*

IRINA   I hope to God it all works out. *(Runs to the window and looks out.)* Isn't it a wonderful day! I don't know why it is but I feel so—so joyous! *(Turning round again.)* I'd forgotten all about my birthday until I woke this morning and suddenly I felt so happy, so happy! I just lay there thinking about when I was young and mama was alive and life was so simple and there was so much happiness; and just to think about them made me so excited again.

OLGA   You really are radiant today. I've never seen you look so beautiful. Masha's beautiful too. And Andrey would be quite handsome if he lost some of that weight. I'm the only one of the four of us that—that's standing the times badly. Oh yes; I know I've become lean and hard—I suppose because those girls at school make me angry so often. But today—today I'm free. Today I'm at home. The migraine's vanished and I feel younger than I felt yesterday. I'm only twenty-eight, amn't I? So. All's well. Everything's in God's good hands. All the same I'd prefer to be married and be at home every day. If I had a husband I would really love him.

BARON TUSENBACH *breaks away from the others and comes down to the drawingroom. As he descends*

BARON   **Talk**-talk-talk. Endless silly talk. That's all they do is talk. I meant to tell you: you're having a visitor today—our new battery commander—Lieutenant Colonel Vershinin.

He sits at the piano and begins playing Won't You Buy My Pretty Flowers? *His playing is heavy and enthusiastic.* MASHA *turns away as if to avoid the sound.*

BARON (*Sings*) 'There are many sad and weary in this pleasant world of ours . . .'

IRINA Oh my God.

OLGA What's his name again?

BARON Vershinin. (*Sings*) 'Crying every night so dreary, Won't you buy my pretty flowers?'

IRINA I'm sure he's ancient.

BARON (*Stops playing*) Sorry?

IRINA I said I'm sure he's ancient.

BARON Somewhere between forty and forty-five. Is that ancient? I think you'll like him. He talks too much but he's a decent man.

IRINA I'm sure he's a bore.

BARON No, he's not a bore! Let's see: he's married—this is his second wife and he has a mother-in-law and two young daughters. You'll hear all about them. He's going round the town making courtesy calls and everyone's being told about 'my wife and my two little girls'. You'll hear about them too. The wife has nervous trouble: wears her hair in a pig-tail like a school-girl and every so often makes a stab at killing herself—just to keep him on his toes, to coin a phrase. If she were my wife I'd have left her years ago. But he endures it. It gives him a valid reason for feeling sorry for himself.

SOLYONY *and* CHEBUTYKIN *come down.* CHEBUTYKIN *is engrossed in his paper and pays no attention to* SOLYONY. *As they descend*

SOLYONY With one hand I can lift only half-a-hundredweight. All right? But with two hands I can lift a hundredweight and a half. So what does that suggest? That two men aren't just twice as strong as one man but

12

| | three times as strong, maybe four or five times as strong. Isn't that a reasonable deduction? |
| CHEBUTYKIN | *(Reads)* 'A cure for alopecia.' That means losing your hair. *(He produces a notebook and pencil.)* Must make a note of this. *(Reads)* 'Mix two ounces of nathphaline with one half-pint of surgical spirits. Apply daily and dissolve.' Apply daily and diss- Shouldn't that be 'Dissolve and apply daily'? What would I write that nonsense for! Rubbish-rubbish-rubbish. |

IRINA runs to him and catches both his hands.

IRINA	Dear, darling, dopey doctor!
CHEBUTYKIN	My own little sweetheart—what is it?
IRINA	You'll know the answer.
CHEBUTYKIN	The answer to what?
IRINA	Why am I so happy today? I feel—I feel as if I had become ethereal—as if I were gliding along with the great blue sky above me and huge white birds all around me!

He kisses her hands tenderly.

CHEBUTYKIN	You're my tiny white bird.
IRINA	D'you know what happened to me this morning just after I'd washed and dressed?
CHEBUTYKIN	Tell me.
IRINA	I had a revelation!
CHEBUTYKIN	Good.
IRINA	A genuine epiphany. Everything made immediate sense. Suddenly I knew how life should be lived. Suddenly I possessed profound wisdom. Are you listening to me, dopey doctor?
CHEBUTYKIN	Avidly. What was the revelation?
IRINA	That man must work. It doesn't matter who he is or what he is. He must toil by the sweat of his brow. Work—work—work; that's the only thing that gives life purpose and meaning. That's the only thing that guarantees contentment and happiness. I'm telling you. My God, what I'd give to be a labourer with the county council, up at the crack of dawn and out smashing stones! Or a sheep-farmer. Or a bus-

driver. Or a teacher slogging away, informing young minds. Isn't that a real revelation? Because if I'm just a slut having my breakfast in bed and lying on till noon and then spending a couple of hours dithering over what I'll wear, then wouldn't I be far better off being a cart-horse or a donkey— anything at all just as long as I can work, work, work. *That's* what life is—work! You know how you'd give anything for a cool drink in the middle of a hot summer day? Well that's exactly what I feel about work—I thirst for it! So from this moment, dopey doctor, if I'm not up at dawn and out there slaving, never ever break breath with me again.

CHEBUTYKIN Never ever. I promise.

OLGA We were all up at seven when father was alive. Irina still wakes at seven but somehow she never manages to rise for at least two more hours. Of course she's thinking. And having revelations.

Everybody laughs.

IRINA You think it's funny when I'm being serious. That's because you persist in looking on me as a child. I am twenty years old today, Olga.

The BARON *gets up from the piano.*

BARON Irina's right. My God how well I know that thirst for work. And why do I know it? I'll tell you why. Because in all my life I've never done a hand's turn! Born in lazy Petersburg. A family that didn't know what work or worry meant. I'd come home from cadet school. A footman to pull off my riding boots. Me making it difficult for him. And mother— mother gazing at me in admiration and actually offended when others didn't find me quite as engaging as she did. The point is: I was *shielded* from work. *But:* we can't be shielded finally. Oh, no. And I'll tell you why: because we are on the threshold of a revolution. To coin a phrase, an avalanche is about to descend on us. A tremendous hurricane is about to rise up. It's close. It's imminent. And what will be the result? All the laziness, complacency, rottenness, boredom, shirking of work—all are going to be purged out of society as we know it now. So not only am I myself absolutely determined to work, but in another twenty-five or thirty years, everyone everywhere—to coin a phrase—will work.

CHEBUTYKIN Except me.

BARON You don't count.

SOLYONY *(Smiling at the* BARON *with icy sweetness)* In twenty-five years time you won't be around, thank God. And I'll tell you why. Some happy day soon you'll have a coronary. Or maybe I'll get really angry with you and—*(He mimes putting a revolver to his head and pulling the trigger)*—phwt! *(Looking around)* When he stands there like that doesn't he remind you of a duck? *(To the* BARON, *softly and with accompanying gesture of his left hand)* Quack-quack, quack-quack, quack-quack.

He takes a bottle of Eau-de-Cologne from his pocket and sprinkles some on his hands.

CHEBUTYKIN Now that I think about it—I've never worked either! Never lifted a finger since the day I graduated! Never even opened a book! The only thing I read now is newspapers. See? But of course I extract lots of very profound information from these same newspapers. For example I see here that there is a critic called — *(Reads)* — Nickolai Dobrolyubov. Now there's an important-sounding name for you! But what Nickolai Dobrolyubov 'criticises' I'm afraid I don't know and I'm afraid I don't care. *(Knocking from below.)* Ah! I'm wanted downstairs. Maybe somebody wants to consult me! *(Calls)* Coming! Coming!

He leaves.

IRINA He's up to something. What is he at?

BARON *(Knowingly)* It wouldn't surprise me if he were away to get your birthday present.

IRINA Oh no. Stop him, Olga.

15

OLGA   'Stop him!' How do you stop a stupid man being stupid?

MASHA   'A green oak grows by a curving shore
And on that oak a gold chain hangs;
And on that oak a gold chain hangs.'

OLGA   You're very quiet today, Masha.

MASHA, *humming, puts on her hat.*

OLGA   Where are you going?

MASHA   Home.

IRINA   'Home!' What d'you mean—'home'?

BARON   Aren't you going to wait for your sister's party?

MASHA   Party? *(Suddenly remembering; to* IRINA*)* Of course. Of course. I'll be back this evening. 'Bye, love. *(Kisses her.)* And once more—all the happiness in the world. *(To everybody)* In the old days when father was alive, we always had thirty or forty young officers here at our birthday parties. Remember the mad fun there used to be? Now we're reduced to one man *(Baron)* and one boy *(Solyony)* and a house as quiet as a library . . . I'm sorry. I'd better go. Pay no attention to me. Sorry I'm so depressed today I almost—I—I'm—*(She laughs through her tears and hugs* IRINA.*)* We'll have a chat later. See you all then. I've got to get out, out, away, somewhere ——

IRINA   Masha, are you sick?

OLGA   *(Crying and embracing* MASHA*)* I know exactly how you feel.

SOLYONY   *(Smiling his icy smile)* When a man attempts to philosophise, the chances are you'll hear something approaching philosophy—or at least a kind of sophistry. But when a woman attempts to philosophise—or better still a pair of women—d'you know what you get? *You* know, Baron. *(The hand gesture and his face close to Tusenbach's face)* Quack-quack, quack-quack, quack-quack.

MASHA   You really are a twisted little pup!

SOLYONY   Me? 'Tweedle-de-dum and tweedle-de-dee, Is there a bird as happy as we?'

MASHA   *(Angrily to* OLGA*)* And will you stop snivelling, Olga!

SOLYONY *crosses the stage with his icy smile, silently miming his duck sounds with his mouth and his left hand. Enter* ANFISA *and* FERAPONT *with a large cake.*

ANFISA Come on, slowcoach—hurry up—move, move, move! Come on, your boots are clean enough. *(To* IRINA*)* Look at this! A birthday cake from Mr. Protopopov!

IRINA *(Puzzled)* Is it for me?

ANFISA Well it's not my birthday. Isn't it lovely! From the county council—from Mr. Protopopov, the chairman.

IRINA *takes the cake.*

IRINA *(To* FERAPONT*)* Thank you. And thank Mister—Mister—

ANFISA Protopopov.

IRINA —thank Mr. Protopopov for me.

FERAPONT Wha's tha', Miss?

IRINA *(Loudly)* Please thank Mr. Protopopov for me.

FERAPONT *is bewildered and looks from* ANFISA *to* IRINA *and back.*

OLGA Give him a cup of tea, Nanny. *(Loudly)* Anfisa will get you something to eat in the kitchen, Ferapont.

FERAPONT Wha's tha', Miss? Wha's tha'?

ANFISA Come on! Come on with me! This way, Ferapont. *(As she leads him off she looks back.)* Old people!

They exit.

MASHA I don't like that Protopopov. He shouldn't be invited here.

IRINA Who's invited him?

MASHA Haven't you?

IRINA Never.

MASHA Good.

CHEBUTYKIN *enters followed by an orderly carrying a silver samovar. A buzz of surprise and dismay at the inappropriateness of the gift.*

OLGA   Would you look at what he's got her! A samovar!
        Oh my God!

IRINA   That's what you give to old maids!

OLGA *goes up to the diningroom and busies herself.*

BARON   *(Laughs)* Didn't I tell you!

IRINA   Darling, dopey doctor, why did you go and do that?

MASHA   Because he's beyond talking to—that's why.

CHEBUTYKIN Because, my dear girls, my darling girls, because
        you're all I have. Because you're more precious to
        me than anything in the world. I'm nearly sixty.
        I'm an old man, a lonely old man, a kind of useless
        old man. But if there's anything good about me,
        it's my love for you three. If it wasn't for you, I—
        I'd—I'd have packed it in long ago. *(Quietly to*
        IRINA) And because I loved your mother—you
        know that, don't you?—loved her with a great,
        great . . . may God have mercy on her soul. And
        because I have loved you since the day you were
        born. When you were a baby—I've told you this
        before, haven't I?—Course I have. *(To all)* I used
        to rock her to sleep in my arms. Yes. Like that.

IRINA   Listen to me: you have just got to stop buying me
        these expensive presents. There's to be no more!

CHEBUTYKIN *(Wiping his eyes and angrily)* Expensive presents!
        Who gives a damn about expense! *(To orderly)*
        Take that bloody thing in there! *(Imitating her)*
        'Expensive presents'!

        *The orderly takes the samovar into the dining-
        room.* ANFISA *enters—carrying a tray.*

ANFISA Colonel Somebody-or-Other has arrived. Never
        clapped eyes on him before. He's taken off his coat
        if you don't mind and he's on his way upstairs.
        Irina, you just behave yourself now, madam.
        (Pause as she goes up to the diningroom.) And I
        suppose you're complaining that your lunch is late.
        Well, I've only one pair of hands, you know!

BARON   It must be Vershinin. *(VERSHININ enters).* It is. *(He
        bows.)* Colonel Vershinin, Sir.

VERSHININ *(To* MASHA) May I introduce myself? My name's

18

Vershinin. It's a great pleasure to be here at last, a very great pleasure. God, how you've changed! My God, I would never ——

Suddenly realising what he is saying he breaks off. An awkward silence.

IRINA   You're very welcome, Colonel. Here—sit down.

VERSHININ   *(With great animation)* It really is a great, great pleasure to see you again. But there were three of you, weren't there? Three sisters? Of course there were. I distinctly remember three little girls, Colonel Prozorov's three little daughters. The faces—they're gone. But that there were three of you—oh, yes, I'm sure of that. *(Indicating three small children)* Where have the years gone to? What happened to them?

BARON   Colonel Vershinin's from Moscow.

IRINA   From Moscow? You're from Moscow!

VERSHININ   Yes. From Moscow. I served in the same brigade as your father when he was battery commander there. *(To MASHA)* There is something about your face that I seem to remember.

MASHA   I've no memory of you.

IRINA   Olga! Olga! Come here, Olga!

OLGA *comes down to the drawingroom.*

IRINA   This is Colonel Vershinin—my sister, Olga. And she's Masha. And I'm Irina. And guess what, Olga! —he's from Moscow!

VERSHININ   Yes, that's where I went to school; that's where I joined up. And I've been stationed there ever since; seems like an eternity. Then this posting came up and I escaped. Actually I don't really remember you. I just remember that there were three sisters. Your father—oh, I remember your father perfectly. *(He mimes a large, straight man.)* Oh, yes, the general I remember vividly. I was a constant visitor in your house in Moscow.

OLGA   And I thought I remembered everybody and every tiny detail. But now—suddenly ——

VERSHININ   Vershinin? Alexander Vershinin? Lieutenant Vershinin in those days?

19

IRINA   And now Colonel Vershinin. And from Moscow. Olga, it's an omen!

VERSHININ   It's a —— ?

OLGA   What she means is—we're moving to Moscow.

IRINA   We'll be there by autumn. That's our home— Moscow. That's where we were born. In Old Basmanny Street.

OLGA and IRINA both laugh.

MASHA   Out of nowhere—someone from home walks in. It's so—*(suddenly and eagerly)*—Yes, I do remember! Olga, d'you remember the man they used to call the Lovesick Major? *(To* VERSHININ*)* That's you! You were a lieutenant then. And you must have been in love. And everyone took a hand at you and called you Major for some reason!

VERSHININ   *(Laughs)* Unmasked! The Lovesick Major—that's me!

MASHA   And you only had a moustache in those days. Yes, I remember that. Lord, how you've aged! *(Through her tears)* Good Lord, how you've aged!

She suddenly realises what she has said. A momentary awkward silence.

VERSHININ   Yes . . . well . . . the Lovesick Major was a young man then, wasn't he? . . . And in love . . . That's all finished now, isn't it?

OLGA   There's not a grey hair in your head. And of course you're older—aren't we all? Nowadays we call that 'a mature look'.

VERSHININ   It would need to be: I'll soon be forty-three. Is it long since you left Moscow?

OLGA
IRINA } *(Together)* Eleven years.

They laugh with embarrassment.

IRINA   Masha, what are you crying for? Goose! *(Beginning to cry)* Now look what you've done: you have me crying, too!

MASHA	Who's crying? Tell me, where did you live in Moscow?
VERSHININ	Old Basmanny Street.
OLGA	That's where we lived!
IRINA	I've told him that, Olga.
VERSHININ	I used to live in Nyemetsky Street. I could walk to the Red Barracks from there. And on the way you had to cross this black bridge and underneath you could just hear the water—a kind of throaty, strangled sound. It was so—hah!—it wasn't the liveliest place to pass on your way to work every morning by yourself. *(Suddenly interest in the view from the window.)* Well, look at that! And the river! Isn't that a really beautiful view!
OLGA	It's cold. It's always cold here. And the midges would devour you.
VERSHININ	Cold? You have the ideal Russian climate here. And you have the forest and the river and—those are silver birches over there, aren't they? Gentle, modest birch trees; they're my favourite. You don't know how lucky you are to be living here. But would someone please explain something to me?
IRINA	What?
VERSHININ	Why is the railway station fifteen miles from the town! Nobody seems to know!
SOLYONY	I do. *(Everybody looks at him.)* Because if the station were here, it wouldn't be fifteen miles away. But that's obvious, isn't it? However, if it were fifteen miles away, as it is—*(Pause)*—then it wouldn't be here, as it isn't.

Solyony's explanation is received in total silence.

BARON	*(To* VERSHININ*)* Solyony's sense of humour is . . . his own.
OLGA	I'm sure I remember you now. I must remember you. Yes. I do.
VERSHININ	I knew your mother well.
CHEBUTYKIN	Their mother? Ah! Their mother . . . May God have mercy on her soul.
IRINA	Mother's buried in Moscow.
OLGA	In the old cemetery.
MASHA	I can hardly remember what she looked like. Isn't

21

that strange? Not that we'll be remembered either. We'll be forgotten, too.

VERSHININ Of course we will. C'est la vie. Nothing you can do about that. Even the big issues we consider so 'serious' today, so 'significant', in time they'll find their true size; maybe they'll be completely forgotten. *(Pause)* The trouble is, we've no way of knowing now what will be thought serious or significant and what will seem frivolous and trivial. Look at Columbus. Look at Copernicus. People dismissed them as cranks. And yet the rubbish spouted by some fool who was a contemporary of theirs—that was hailed as—as—as a revelation! God alone knows how the way we live will be assessed. To us it's—it's how we live, our norm. But maybe in retrospect it will look anxious and tense. Maybe even . . . morally wrong. Well . . .

He spreads his hands in dismissal of his solemnity.

BARON If I understand you correctly I think you have a point. On the other hand perhaps our age will be called a great age and looked back on with admiration, to coin a phrase. I mean to say we've no torture chambers, no public executions, no invasions. Of course on the other hand one must admit that there is still a totally unacceptable level of human suffering and ——

SOLYONY Quack-quack, quack-quack, quack-quack. Our Baron's a philosopher, a real ideas man. *(Close into Tusenbach's face)* 'To coin a phrase', a totally unacceptable level of what?

BARON Leave me alone, Solyony. *(Moves away)* I'm asking you. Please.

SOLYONY *(Smiling, softly)* Quack-quack. *(Then two more quacks in mime.)*

BARON The point I'm trying to make is simply this: that the misery we see around us—and God knows I deplore it as much as anybody—but the fact that it is *only* misery and not actual—*(out of the corner of his eye he sees* SOLYONY *miming a quack-quack at him and his line of thought is gone)*—that would seem

	to suggest—wouldn't you agree?—that—that ——
VERSHININ	I've no idea what you're saying.
BARON	What I'm suggesting is that that would seem to argue —the fact that it is no worse than misery—that our society has in fact developed to a slightly higher plane of moral awareness and sensitivity than obtained . . . a higher level of morality than that same society, in other words *this* society, had reached—has reached—is now—is . . . *(He is lost.)*
CHEBUTYKIN	I know what your point is, Tusenbach.
BARON	Thank you, doctor.
CHEBUTYKIN	This is a great era. It's just people who are small. And you're right. *(He rises and stands to his full height.)* Right? Not the height of tuppence. But all you have to do is *tell* me I live in a great age and I'll believe I'm a giant.

Sound of a violin being played off.

VERSHININ	You have a musician in the house?
MASHA	That's Andrey, our brother.
IRINA	Andrey's the brains of the family. He's going to be an academic.
MASHA	That was father's wish.
IRINA	No interest at all in the army. We think he's destined for a brilliant career as a university professor.
OLGA	In the meantime we think he's in love. We've been teasing him all morning.
IRINA	She's a local girl. You'll probably meet her later.
MASHA	Indeed you will, with her poor-but-honest provincial face. And be dazzled by her yellows and greens and purples.
OLGA	She dresses . . . distinctively.
MASHA	I know nobody who risks so many startling combinations of colours. I'm afraid Miss Natasha's taste is . . . peccable.
OLGA	She's ——
MASHA	Vulgar, for God's sake! Plain, downright vulgar! Andrey in love with her! Come on, Olga; he's got some discrimination. *He's* teasing *us*. In fact I know he is: somebody told me yesterday she's going with that Protopopov creature, the chairman of the

23

county council. It sounds a perfect match. They're welcome to one another. *(She crosses to a door right.)* Andrey, have you a moment? Could you come out for a moment, Andrey?

> ANDREY *emerges awkwardly, his face half-averted.* MASHA *hugs him warmly. He is in his twenties; plump; thick glasses; very shy. He is both cossetted and overwhelmed by his three affectionate and garrulous sisters.*

MASHA Our Tchaikovsky!
OLGA This is our brother, Andrey.
VERSHININ My name's Vershinin.
ANDREY My name's Prozorov.

> *Pause.* ANDREY *mops his face with his handkerchief. Nobody speaks. Then simultaneously*

VERSHININ ⎱ I was ——
ANDREY ⎰ You're just ——

> *Again a silence. Then*

VERSHININ Sorry?
ANDREY You're the new battery commander here, aren't you?
OLGA Colonel Vershinin's from Moscow, Andrey! Isn't that wonderful?
ANDREY Yes? Ah. Well. In that case God help you. You won't get a moment's peace from my darling sisters.
VERSHININ I'm afraid your darling sisters are already bored with me.
IRINA Look what Andrey gave me today—this little picture frame. *(She hands it to* VERSHININ.*)* He made it himself.

> VERSHININ *looks at the frame. He does not know what to say.*

VERSHININ Well. That—that's very—that would certainly— frame a picture, wouldn't it?

IRINA And you see the one on top of the piano? He made that too.

ANDREY *makes an impatient gesture and moves away.*

OLGA Andrey's a scholar and a musician and an artist. He has all the talents. No slipping away, Andrey. *(To* VERSHININ*)* That's typical of him. Come back here, Andrey!

MASHA *and* IRINA *run after him and arrest him. Laughing they lead him back to the centre of the room.*

MASHA No, no, no you don't.
ANDREY Please . . . please . . . please . . .
IRINA *(Child's chant)* 'Andrey is huffing/Andrey is huffing.'
ANDREY Please . . .
MASHA They used to call Alexander the Lovesick Major and he didn't huff—did you?
VERSHININ Never!
MASHA So I'm going to christen you the Lovesick Fiddler.
IRINA The Lovesick Professor.
OLGA Poor little Andrey's in love. Are you passionately in love, Andrey?

By now the three girls have encircled him and dance around him, repeating: 'Andrey is huffing/ Andrey is huffing' *and* 'The Lovesick Fiddler' *and* 'Poor little Andrey. What does it feel like, little Andrey?' *And now* CHEBUTYKIN *comes up from behind and puts his arm round Andrey's waist.*

CHEBUTYKIN 'For love alone did nature make us
That it might bend and try to break us.'

CHEBUTYKIN *returns to his chair and his paper.* ANDREY *breaks away from his sisters.*

ANDREY Alright-alright-alright-alright. Come on. That's enough. A joke's a joke. Please . . . please . . . *(He wipes the perspiration off his face.)* I'm not feeling

25

	too well today. Didn't close an eye all night. I sat up studying till four and then when I went to bed my mind was too active ——
IRINA	*(Coyly)* Ah-ha!
ANDREY	—— and I just couldn't sleep. Then when I was about to drop off, suddenly it's daylight and the sun's pouring in the damned window.
VERSHININ	What are you studying?
ANDREY	An English text, a thing I'm hoping to translate over the summer.
VERSHININ	Do you know English?
ANDREY	Yes. Oh, yes. And French. And German. We all do—don't we? Irina's fluent in Italian too. A liberal education, painfully acquired. You see, father—God have mercy on him—father had a mania about 'learning'. 'The lightest load you'll ever carry' he used to say. I know it sounds ridiculous but as soon as he died I began to put on weight, just as if I'd been physically relieved of a burden. *(Laughs uneasily)* And I haven't stopped, have I? Fatter by the hour. Oh, yes. The Prozorov children are all competent linguists.
MASHA	And you can imagine how useful it is to be able to speak three languages in a town like this! It's almost a necessity, isn't it? Like having eleven toes or a sixth finger. Hah! Nearly everything we know is . . . useless.
VERSHININ	Oh, come on! 'Useless'? *(Laughs)* That's just not true. Educated, intelligent people are valuable in every community, even more valuable in a place like this in the back of beyond. What's the population of this town? 100,000? And there are three of you. Three Prozorovs encircled by 100,000 ignorant, uneducated people. Well of course you're not going to transform 100,000 people. Of course you'll be eroded bit by bit, day by day, until finally the 100,000 will overwhelm you. But the fact that you're swallowed up—and you will be, make no mistake about that—that doesn't mean you'll have made no impact. Because you will. You'll have influenced perhaps—let's be modest, let's say six other people. And in turn those six will influence twelve more. And that twelve another twenty-four.

Until finally, finally people like you will be in the majority. Until finally in two or three hundred years time the quality of life on this earth will be transformed and beautiful and marvellous beyond our imagining. Because *that's* the life man longs for and aspires to. And even though he hasn't achieved it yet, he must fashion it in his imagination, look forward to it, dream about it, prepare for it. But he can fashion it in his imagination and prepare for it only if he has more vision and more knowledge than his father or his grandfather. *(Again he spreads his hands in embarrassment and apology.)* Well . . . *(Laughs. To* MASHA*)* Just because you said that nearly everything you know is . . . what was it?—'useless'?

> *Pause.* MASHA *looks at him. Then still looking at him she resolutely takes off her hat.*

MASHA   I'm staying for lunch.

IRINA   *(To* VERSHININ; *in awe)* Do you know something? Every word you've said should be written down.

> ANDREY *has slipped away unnoticed.*

BARON   If I understand you correctly, your point is that in some future time life on this earth will be beautiful and marvellous. That is possible. *But:* if we are to have a part in it now, even vicariously, even at this distance, we must prepare for it, we must work for it, to coin a phrase we must ——

VERSHININ   *(Cutting him off)* Indeed. My God I've never seen so many flowers. The whole place—it's so elegant; it has the taste of women about it. I envy you. I seem to spend my life flitting from one shabby flat to another. A couple of chairs, a camp bed, a stove that always seems to smoke. Flowers! That's what's been missing from my life! Flowers like these!

BARON   No doubt about it—work is the answer. We've just got to get down to real hard work. And if you think that's just Baron Tusenbach indulging in German sentimentality, you're wrong. Despite the name I'm one hundred per cent Russian. Don't even speak a word of German. In point of fact my father was a practising Orthodox long before ——

VERSHININ *(Walking around the room)* Did you ever wonder what it would be like if you could begin your life over again—with the knowledge that you have now? Supposing you could put aside the life you've already lived, as if it were just a try-out, and then start the other one, the *real* life. D'you know the first thing you'd do? You'd make absolutely sure you wouldn't repeat yourself. You'd try to create a different environment for yourself: a house like this, spacious, lots of light, flowers, the taste of women about it . . . I should have told you. I'm married. I've two little girls. My wife is . . . delicate. Not that all that has anything to do with . . . But as I say, the first rule must be: never repeat yourself. Oh, no. Never. Never.

Enter KULYGIN *wearing a schoolteacher's uniform.*

KULYGIN Ah! The birthday-girl herself! May I wish you, dear Irina, from the bottom of my heart may I wish you a most happy occasion; many, many felicitous repetitions of it in the future; and whatever a young lady of your age may wish for herself—and I suspect that may well be robust good health—am I right? There! And may I present to you this little volume. *(Hands her a book.)* A history of our secondary school, covering the past fifty years. Written by yours truly. A modest little enterprise executed in moments of leisure but still worth a casual perusal. Good afternoon, everybody! *(To* VERSHININ*)* Kulygin's the name. By profession a teacher in the local secondary school. And for my sins a humble member of the county council. *(To* IRINA*)* Basically it consists of lists of all the pupils who have passed through our hands in the last fifty years. *Feci quod potui; faciant meliora potentes.* In other words: I have done what I can; let those with more talent do better. *(He kisses* MASHA.*)*

IRINA You gave me a copy of this last Easter, Fyodor.

KULYGIN *(Laughs)* I didn't—did I? In that case give it back to me or, better still, give it to the colonel. *(He*

	presents it to VERSHININ.*)* There you are, Colonel. Have a look at it some time when you've nothing better to do.
VERSHININ	Thank you. *(Preparing to leave.)* I'm very glad to have met you all and ——
OLGA	You're not leaving already, are you? What's the hurry?
IRINA	Stay and have lunch with us. Please.
OGLA	Yes; have your lunch here. It's all ready.
VERSHININ	I feel I've intruded on a family ——
OGLA	Please.
VERSHININ	Well . . .

He looks directly at MASHA. *She holds his look for a second; then turns away.*

| VERSHININ | Why not! I'd love to. And a very happy birthday, Irina. |

He and OLGA *go into the diningroom.*

| KULYGIN | Sunday, gentlemen! The day of rest! And because it is the day of rest what we must all do is . . . rest! Relax and enjoy ourselves with as much brio as each of us is capable. Those carpets will have to be lifted for the summer and put away until next winter. Must remember to get mothballs or naphthaline; they're equally effective. Why were the Romans a healthy people? The Romans were a healthy people because they knew how to work *and* how to rest. They had in consequence *mens sana in corpore sano.* In other words: a healthy mind in a healthy body. Their life had shape, form. And as our headmaster says, he says: the most important thing in every life is its form; that which loses its form cannot survive. And look around you. Isn't he right? *(He puts his arm around Masha's waist and laughs.)* Masha loves me. Yes. My wife loves me. Yes. And we must put those winter curtains away with the carpets. I'm really happy today; joyous in fact. Masha, we're invited to the headmaster's house at four this afternoon. An outing has been arranged for the teachers and their families. |

MASHA   I'm not going.

KULYGIN   *(Hurt)* My darling—why not?

MASHA   We'll talk about it later.

KULYGIN   But arrangements have all been ——

MASHA   *(Angrily)* All right—I'll go—I'll go! But for God's sake leave me alone now, will you . . . please . . .

She moves away from him.

KULYGIN   And after the outing we'll spend the rest of the evening with the headmaster. Despite his indifferent health he is a man of unfailing sociability, of enormous integrity, of enviable perspicacity. Do you know what he said to me after the staff meeting yesterday? What he said to me was this: 'Kulygin,' he said, 'Kulygin, I am tired.' *(He looks at the clock and then at his watch.)* Your clock is seven minutes fast. Yes; those were his precise words—'I am tired.'

Sounds of the violin being played off stage.

OLGA   Come and eat, everybody! The lasagne's going cold.

KULYGIN   Coming, Olga! Yesterday I worked from early morning until almost midnight and I can tell you I was just spent. But today? Exuberant! The most wonderful thing about the human spirit is its resilience.

He goes up to the diningroom.

CHEBUTYKIN   Did I hear someone say lasagne? I'm a great lasagne man.

He puts away his paper and combs his beard.

MASHA   Remember—just because it's a birthday doesn't mean you can take a drink.

CHEBUTYKIN   Me? Drink?

MASHA   You know you can't handle it.

CHEBUTYKIN   I've been dry for five hundred and ninety seven and a half days now.

MASHA   For your own good.

CHEBUTYKIN 'My own good'! Who gives a damn about that, my love? Who gives a tinker's damn?

MASHA I do. And well you know it.

She takes his arm. She speaks softly and angrily.

MASHA Another bloody boring evening at the headmaster's! Bloody hell!

BARON What's the problem? If I were you I just wouldn't go.

CHEBUTYKIN He's right, my love. Don't go.

MASHA 'Don't go'! Hah! Oh damn this—this—this bloody, dreary, grinding life!

She goes up to the diningroom. CHEBUTYKIN *follows her.*

CHEBUTYKIN Easy, my love, easy . . .

As SOLYONY *passes the* BARON.

SOLYONY *(Barely audible)* Quack-quack, quack-quack.

BARON Leave me alone, Solyony. I'm asking you. Please.

SOLYONY *responds with his left-hand mime and his icy smile. Only* IRINA *and* BARON TUSENBACH *are left in the drawingroom.*

KULYGIN Your very good health, Colonel. And welcome. I'm Masha's husband—did I mention that? A schoolteacher by profession and happily by inclination and, if I may say so myself, very much an integral part of the household here. As for Masha, my wife, Masha I may say is the very personification of kindness and consideration and loyalty and circumspection and ——

VERSHININ I'll try some of this dark vodka, I think. *(Toast)* To the Prozorov family. *(To* OLGA*)* I'm very happy to be here with you all.

Welcoming sounds. General talk. OLGA *serves the meal.*

IRINA   (*To* TUSENBACH*)* Masha's in bad form today. She was only eighteen when they got married; and at that age he probably seemed the cleverest man in the world. Things have changed. He's a very kind man but hardly the cleverest.

OLGA   Andrey! Are you coming or are you not!

ANDREY   *(Off)* Coming.

He enters and goes straight to the table.

BARON   What are you thinking about?

IRINA   Nothing much . . . just that I don't like your friend, Solyony. There's something sinister about him. I think I'm frightened of him.

BARON   He's an odd fish. I'm equally sorry for him and irritated by him. No, that's not accurate. I'm more sorry than irritated. I think he's shy. When we're alone together he's quite normal—very relaxed, even warm. But when there are others around he becomes aggressive and —— (IRINA *moves towards the diningroom.*) Don't go in yet. Wait till they've all sat down. Let me—let me just stand beside you for a while. *(Pause)* What are you thinking about? *(Pause)* You're only twenty and I'm not thirty yet and stretching out before us, waiting for us, are all those years—days and days to be filled with my love for you and ——

IRINA   Please—please don't talk like that. I ——

BARON   I'm exercised by two great passions: one is my thirst for life, for work, for challenges; the other is my love for you. And somehow these two passions have fused and become one: life is beautiful because *you* are so beautiful. What are you thinking about?

IRINA   'Life is beautiful'—you say it so easily. Is it beautiful? Maybe it is. Life for us three sisters hasn't been very 'beautiful' so far, has it? *(She is fingering flowers in a vase and now picks out a withered one.)* Life can stifle, too, you know. Look—it never got a chance to blossom. And now I'm crying. Stupid, amn't I? *(She hurriedly wipes away her tears and tries to smile.)* What we must do is work, and work, and work. If we're depressed it's because we don't

know what the word work means; and we don't
know what it means because we're descended from
people who despised work.

NATASHA *enters wearing a pink dress and a green
sash*

NATASHA   Sweet mother of God, I'm late—they're at the
dinner already! *(Quick look in the mirror. She
adjusts her hair.)* It'll have to do now. *(She sees
IRINA and goes to her. Her accent becomes slightly
posh.)* Irina darling, many many happy returns.
(She gives IRINA a vigorous and prolonged kiss.)
And look at the crowd of guests! Goodness gracious
I could never face in there! Baron, how d'you do.

OLGA *comes down from the diningroom.*

OLGA   Ah, Natasha's here. How are you, Natasha?
NATASHA   As my mother used to say, 'Never felt better and
had less'—ha-ha-ha. *(They kiss)* God but that's a
wild big crowd, Olga. I could never face that
crowd.
OLGA   Of course you can. They're our friends. *(Quietly)*
And you're wearing a green sash. That's . . .
unusual.
NATASHA   You mean it's unlucky, Olga? Because it's green?
Is it a bad omen, Olga?
OLGA   Not at all. It's just that against the pink it—it—it's
quite . . . distinctive.
NATASHA   *(Tearfully)* You're right. It's wrong. But it's not
really a greeny green, is it? Like I mean it's more a
sort of kind of neutral green, isn't it?

*She follows OLGA into the diningroom. The draw-
ingroom is now empty.*

KULYGIN   And now, Irina, what you have got to do is seek out
an eligible young man for yourself. Because in my
opinion—for what that's worth—it's time you were
contemplating matrimony.
CHEBUTYKIN   Isn't it time Natasha found herself an eligible young
man too?

KULYGIN   My spies tell me that Natasha has already found her man. Am I correct, Natasha?

MASHA *deliberately drops her plate on the table.*

MASHA   I want some wine! Why are you keeping the bloody wine hidden up there?

KULYGIN   Oh-ho! Language, Masha, language! Black mark, my darling.

VERSHININ   Here. Try this. This is very good. What is it made of?

SOLYONY   Crushed cockroaches.

IRINA   My God you're disgusting.

OLGA   Tonight we're having roast turkey and apple pie for dinner. I'm free as the wind today and I'm going to do all the cooking myself. So I want you all to join us again tonight.

VERSHININ   *(To* MASHA*)* Does that include me?

IRINA   Of course it includes you.

VERSHININ   Good.

NATASHA   *(Coyly)* We don't stand on ceremony in this house, do we?

CHEBUTYKIN   *(Into Andrey's ear)* 'For love alone did nature make us/That it might bend and try to break us.' *(Laughs.)*

ANDREY   *(Angrily)* For God's sake! Do you never get sick of your own jokes?

Enter FEDOTIK *and* RODDEY, *two young lieutenants. Between them they are carrying an enormous wicker basket full of flowers.* FEDOTIK *also carries a camera mounted on a tripod and* RODDEY *a guitar.* RODDEY *speaks with an affected lisp.*

FEDOTIK   We're late. They've already begun.

RODDEY   Oh, my! You're right, my petal. We *are* late.

FEDOTIK *mounts his camera.*

FEDOTIK   Look this way everybody, please!

A response from the group—a mixture of surprise and delight and embarrassment. FEDOTIK *disappears behind his black cloth.*

RODDEY I think they're all just lovely!
FEDOTIK Only take a second. Big smile. Come on—you can
do better than that! Smile. Andrey! Smile! Yes!
Lovely! Terrific!

*He takes his picture—a puff of smoke from his
camera. A response to this.*

FEDOTIK Don't move—one more—just one more. That's it.
Hold it there. That's perfect.
RODDEY They all look just divine, don't they?
FEDOTIK What are the sad faces for? Come on, birthday girl!
That's more like it. Terrific! Terrific!

*Another puff of smoke. Laughter. Clapping. The
group begins to break up.* RODDEY *and* FEDOTIK
*go up to the diningroom where they are greeted
noisily.*

RODDEY Irina, my petal, many, many happy returns and may
all your sweet little dreams come true. And what a
day for a birthday! Magnificent, my petal, isn't it?
You'd never guess where I've been all morning—out
with the boys from the secondary school! Jogging—
as we call it!
IRINA Roddey, you're ——!
RODDEY I'm their instructor in physical education—didn't
you know?

*Another puff of smoke—*FEDOTIK *has taken a
picture of* IRINA *alone.*

FEDOTIK Thank you, Irina. That's all. Relax now. My God
you're looking terrific today.
RODDEY *(Dryly)* We all know that. Now go away and snap
somebody else.

FEDOTIK *is fumbling in his pockets.*

FEDOTIK Wo-wo-wo-wo-wo-wo. *(Produces a tiny top.)* Here
we are. Happy birthday. A top.
IRINA A what?
FEDOTIK Top. A top. A spinning top. A top that . . . spins.

35

IRINA	*(Puzzled)* Thank you, Fedotik.
FEDOTIK	Look. This is how you work it. Terrific.

He demonstrates.

MASHA	'A green oak grows by a curving shore And on that oak a gold chain hangs; And on that oak a gold chain . . .' Why do I keep saying that? Those damn lines have been haunting me all day.
KULYGIN	Ah-hah! Thirteen at table!
RODDEY	Good heavens he's superstitious! You're surely not superstitious, my petal, are you?

Laughter.

KULYGIN	If there are thirteen at table it means that somebody's in love. It wouldn't be yourself, doctor, would it?

Laughter.

CHEBUTYKIN	Me? I'm past all that. But Natasha's a fine healthy colour. Now why's that, Natasha?

Loud laughter. NATASHA *rushes down to the drawingroom.* ANDREY *follows her. As he does*

ANDREY	Natasha—please—don't listen to them —— *(They are now both in the drawingroom.)* Wait—please—wait—don't go away ——
NATASHA	*(Crying)* What the hell did I do that for—making an eejit of myself before everybody. *(To* ANDREY*)* Because they make fun of me all the time—that's the why! I know it was shocking bad manners—I know that!—but I couldn't help myself, Andrey. Honest to God I just couldn't—I couldn't—I couldn't ——

She covers her face with her hands.

ANDREY	Shhhhh, my darling, shh-shh-shh. Please don't cry. Please. They were only teasing; they meant no

harm. My darling, please, please. They're good, good, generous people. They're fond of us both; I know they are. Come over here to the window. They can't see us there.

NATASHA I'm just not used to mixing with posh people like ——

ANDREY Posh! Oh my God, you're so innocent, so beautifully, so magnificently innocent. Don't cry. Please don't cry. If you only knew—if I could only tell you—how I feel about you. I'm wildly in love with you. I'm so in love with you I'm—I'm—I'm besotted by you. *(He takes her in his arms.)* We can't be seen now. *(As he kisses her face and hair and neck.)* Where did we meet? How did I come to fall in love with you? When did it happen? I don't know. I know nothing any more. All I know is that I love you, love you, love you more than I've ever loved anyone in my life before. Will you marry me, my beautiful innocent? Please, will you marry me?

They kiss. As they kiss FEDOTIK *and* RODDEY *come down to the drawingroom and stare at them.*

RODDEY Oh my goodness me! Just look at those two happy petals!

QUICK BLACK. END OF ACT ONE

ACT TWO

It is now late January, over a year and a half later; a Thursday night. The same scene as in Act One. The stage, now bare and empty without the flowers, is in darkness. In the far distance a girl hums Won't You Buy My Pretty Flowers? *and is accompanied by a piano accordion. The music is slow and haunting and sad. A quick brief gust of howling wind and* NATASHA *enters. Her hair in curlers, wearing a house-coat, carrying a candle. She crosses the stage and stops at the door of Andrey's room.*

NATASHA   Andrey, what are you doing, Andrey? *(She opens his door and puts her head in.)* Are you reading? It's all right—don't stir—don't stir—I'm only checking.

> *She closes the door, goes to an adjoining door, opens it, peers in, closes it again.* ANDREY *emerges with a book in his hand.*

ANDREY   What *are* you at, Natasha?

NATASHA   Just having a look around in case the servants might have left a light burning. Maids! You couldn't watch them these days. And this carnival week has them astray in the head altogether. D'you hear? Singing in the streets! Have people no homes to go to? D'you know what I found last night in there? On the table? A candle! A burning candle! At midnight! But who left it burning there? Oh, nobody, nobody! What time is it?

ANDREY   *(Checks watch)* A quarter past eight.

NATASHA   Sweet mother of God, it's not—is it? *(She fingers her curlers briefly, anxiously.)* And poor Olga and Irina aren't even back from work yet, the creatures. Olga has a staff meeting, I think, and this is one of Irina's late nights at the post-office. I was just saying to Irina this very morning, 'You really would need to take better care of yourself, darling'—that's what I said, not that your sister heeds the likes of me. What did you say? A quarter past eight? It's little Bobik—that's what has me all through-other. He's not well, not well at all. One minute he's cold and the next he's sweating like a pig. My stomach's just sick with worry.

ANDREY	There's nothing wrong with Bobik, Natasha. The child's perfectly healthy.
NATASHA	He is—isn't he? All the same I must pack more food into him. God, I worry so much about him. And I'm told we're having a group of mummers calling in about nine on their way to the carnival. It would be better if they didn't come, Andrey.
ANDREY	Why would it? What I mean is—they've been invited and ——
NATASHA	When the wee darling woke up this morning, d'you know what he did? He opened his eyes and he looked straight up at me—and he *smiled!* Honest to God! He knew me! 'Morning, Bobik', I said. 'Morning, my darling little gosling'. And d'you know what he did then? He *laughed!* True as I'm standing here. They understand, you know. They understand everything. What I'll do then, Andrey, is, I'll just tell the maid not to let the mummers in.
ANDREY	But my sisters—I mean, they invited them—and after all this is their house ——
NATASHA	Yes, it's their house, too. I'll have a word with them; they're *very* understanding.

She moves off, forgetting the candle burning on the table. ANDREY *lifts it as if to offer it to her, but with typical irresolution leaves it down again on the table.*

NATASHA	You're having omelette for supper. The doctor says you must eat nothing but omelettes or you'll never lose weight. D'you know why Bobik's always cold? —that damp room he's in! We've got to shift him, at least until the weather's warmer. Irina's room— that would be just perfect for him! She can go in with Olga for the time being. Anyhow she's out all day long. She only sleeps there. *(Pause)* Andrey, love, why don't you say something?
ANDREY	What is there to say? There's nothing to say, is there?
NATASHA	There was something else in my head . . . Yes, Ferapont's here from the county council offices. He wants to see you.
ANDREY	*(Wearily)* Tell him to come up.

She leaves. ANDREY *sits at the table and reads by the light of the candle.* FERAPONT *enters encased in heavy, woollen, shabby clothes. A scarf around his ears.*

ANDREY   Over here, Ferapont. What do you want now?

FERAPONT   The chairman sent you these, the minute book and some papers.

He hands over the book and papers.

ANDREY   Good man. Thank you. You're working late, aren't you? It's almost nine o'clock.

FERAPONT   Wha's that, Sir?

ANDREY   It's almost nine o'clock. You're working late.

FERAPONT   Aye, it's late, Sir, isn't it? But I've been here since before dark only she wouldn't let me in. She said you were busy.

ANDREY   Who said ——

FERAPONT   But sure I know myself you're a busy man. And sure I'm not rushing off to the festival dance in the marquee hee-hee-hee—*(He stops suddenly thinking* ANDREY *has said something.)* Wha's that, Sir?

ANDREY   *(Leafing through the minute book)* Nothing . . . nothing . . . This is Thursday, isn't it? There won't be a meeting until next week. But I might as well go in tomorrow and write these up, I suppose. It will be at least as exciting as moping about here. *(Directly to* FERAPONT *but very quietly)* I'll tell you something, Ferapont: life is a great deceiver. Now there's a profundity for you. I was foothering about in my room today, killing time, keeping out of the way, and look what I came across—*(holds up a book)*—my old university lectures! Go ahead and laugh, man, hee-hee-hee. That's what I did. Andrey Prozorov, part-time clerk in the county council, temporary secretary to Mister Protopopov, the chairman, but with reasonable expectations of being made permanent—oh, yes, Andrey Prozorov still has ambitions. Andrey Prozorov aspires to be made a full-time local government employee. Oh, yes. And every night, Ferapont, every single night in life that same part-time Andrey Prozorov dreams the same dream. He dreams that he is Professor Andrey Prozorov of Moscow University, the distinguished academician, one of Russia's leading intellectuals. Oh, Christ . . .

Pause. FERAPONT *sees he has stopped talking.*

FERAPONT No point in asking me, Sir. Sure I don't hear hardly nothing any more.

ANDREY *(Softly)* If you could hear me, Ferapont, I wouldn't be talking to you. But I must talk to somebody— 'to coin a phrase'. And to coin another phrase— 'My wife doesn't understand me.' And for some reason I'm afraid of the girls, yes, afraid. Ridiculous, isn't it? Afraid they'll laugh at me . . . *(Loudly)* D'you know where I'd love to be at this very moment? In the restaurant of the Great Moscow Hotel! Or better still in Tyestov's Grill Room! Not eating, not drinking, just sitting there.

FERAPONT There was a building contractor in the office the other day and he told me this story and he swears it's true. Two Moscow businessmen went into this eating-house. The first fella he orders forty pancakes. Devours the lot. The second fella looks at him. Orders fifty pancakes. Devours his pile. *(Pause)* The second fella dropped dead hee-hee-hee . . .

ANDREY You can sit in any of the bigger Moscow restaurants and even though you know nobody and nobody knows you you still don't feel you're alone. But here, where you know everyone and everybody knows you, somehow you don't belong at all.

FERAPONT That same contractor told me another thing.

ANDREY *(Not listening)* Yes?

FERAPONT He says there's a huge rope stretched right across Moscow!

ANDREY There's a what?

FERAPONT Stretched right across the whole city, a great, big, long rope.

ANDREY What in God's name for?

FERAPONT A rope—a big, big rope—right across Moscow. That's what the man said.

ANDREY What man?

41

FERAPONT	D'you think was he taking a hand at me?
ANDREY	Have you ever been in Moscow, Ferapont?
FERAPONT	Me! Oh, God, no. Moscow? Oh, never, never. If it had been the will of God I would have been, though. But there you are.
ANDREY	All right. Off you go.
FERAPONT	Wha's that?
ANDREY	Thank you. Good night. *(ANDREY rises.)* Come back tomorrow morning. I'll be finished with these by then.
FERAPONT	Wha's that, Sir? Wha's that?
ANDREY	Good night. Good night. Good night. *(FERAPONT goes.)* Oh my God . . .

ANDREY goes into his room. Off stage a nurse is singing a lullaby to BOBIK. MASHA and VERSHININ enter, shaking the snow off their coats. A maid lights candles and a lamp in the diningroom.

MASHA	I don't know—maybe you *are* right—maybe there is no significant difference between army people and civilians. I suppose it's a question of what you're most used to. I remember after father's death we couldn't get used to the idea that we hadn't a houseful of orderlies to wait on us!
VERSHININ	I'm very thirsty.
MASHA	No, you're wrong, there *is* a difference. Maybe other provincial towns aren't as dead as this one. But in this town the only courteous, the only civilised people are the military. I'm telling you. I live here.
VERSHININ	I'd love a cup of tea.
MASHA	Look at me for example.
VERSHININ	Happily.

He reaches out to hold her. She moves away.

MASHA	You're not listening. I got married when I was eighteen and at that age I was—damnit, yes!—I was in awe of Fyodor because he was a teacher and I'd only just left school myself. I thought he was clever, important, a man of some significance. I did! Wasn't I mature?

VERSHININ You are ——

Again he tries to hold her. Again she eludes him.

MASHA How did we get into this conversation? Civilians! Anyhow what I'm saying is that most of them are coarse, ill-mannered . . . thicks! I can't stand their rudeness! I can't stand their boorishness! I can't stand their ignorance! You've never been in a group of teachers, have you? You've never spent an evening with Fyodor's colleagues? Hah! That's something you must experience!

VERSHININ All I tried to say was ——

MASHA *(Laughs)* That you want a cup of tea!

VERSHININ I happened to make the modest suggestion that people everywhere—this town, any other town, civilian, military—they all have one thing in common: they are all equally dreary. Talk to any soldier, any civilian who's capable of looking objectively at his life, and what will he tell you? That he's sick and tired of it all. Sick and tired of his wife, his family, his home, his job—the whole thing. We Russians are a people whose aspirations are magnificent; it's just living we can't handle. *(His usual embarrassment. He spreads his hands.)* Well . . .

MASHA And why can't we?

VERSHININ Am I the one to ask? Sick and tired of his wife. Sick and tired of his children. And his wife and his children they're equally sick and tired of him.

MASHA *catches his hand.*

MASHA You're in bad form today.

VERSHININ I've had nothing to eat since breakfast! *(He kisses her hand and holds it against his cheek.)* One of the girls is sick. When anything's wrong with them I get so . . . I feel guilty about them and responsible to them because of their mother's condition, as if it were *all* my fault. You should have seen her this morning; she really is a vixen. The fighting began at seven, earlier than usual. Went on and on and on and on. Finally about nine I walked out and

43

slammed the door. *(Again he kisses her hands. Pause.)* Funny thing is, you're the only one I've ever talked to about it. Do you realise how privileged you are to hear my . . . my whinings? *(Kisses her again.)* I've no one, Masha, no one in the world apart from you.

Pause.

MASHA The wind's howling in the stove. It made a noise like that too just before father died.

VERSHININ Are you superstitious?

MASHA Yes. Very.

VERSHININ That's not like you. *(Suddenly he kisses her hands rapidly and repeatedly.)* You're the most wonderful woman I've ever known. Wonderful and marvellous! Even though it's dark your eyes are luminous.

She moves away from him.

MASHA There's more light here.

He goes to her and holds her in his arms.

VERSHININ I love you, Masha, love you, love you, love you. I love your eyes. I love the way you move. Everything, everything you do is wonderful, marvellous, marvellous, wonderful!

MASHA *(Laughing softly)* When you talk to me like that, somehow I can't help laughing even though I'm frightened at the same time. So please don't . . . *(Very softly)* Yes, do; do. *(She covers her face with her hands.)* Please do. I want you to. Yes, do . . . *(A long kiss. Then suddenly she breaks away.)* Somebody's coming!

IRINA *and* TUSENBACH *enter the diningroom.*

BARON All right—I *have* a triple-barrelled name: Baron Tusenbach-Krone-Altschauer. Agreed. *But:* I was baptized in the Greek Orthodox church and I'm every bit as Russian as you are. Not a trace of German ancestry in me except in the way I persist in leaving you home every evening, boringly, predictably, 'Teutonically'.

IRINA God, I'm exhausted.

BARON And I will persist in calling for you at the post-office every day. I'll keep it up for ten years. I'll keep it up for twenty years until you *order* me out of your life. *(Seeing* MASHA *and* VERSHININ*)* Ah. And how are you two?

IRINA Home at last. *(She flops exhausted into a seat.)* Wait till you hear. We're just about to close up when in comes this country woman, a real peasant woman. Wants to send a telegram to her brother to tell him that her son died today. Where does this brother live? In Saratov. Where in Saratov? No idea. Saratov town or Saratov county? Didn't know. Just Saratov. So off it went without an address—just to Saratov! And she was crying all the time. And I was so bitchy with her. 'You're wasting my time, dear', I said. 'My time'! My God. And the moment she shuffled away I wanted to . . . *(She leaps to her feet, suddenly brisk.)* Well, at least we're having the mummers tonight, aren't we?

MASHA Yes.

IRINA *(Weary again)* I must lie down for a while. I'm falling apart. *(She sits.)*

BARON *(With enormous vigour, to* MASHA*)* Did you ever advert to the fact that when she comes home from work she always looks very, very young and very, very vulnerable? Doesn't she?

IRINA *(Eyes closed)* Weary . . . weary . . . weary . . . I hate working in that place. I really do hate it.

MASHA You've lost weight, Irina. You do look younger, sort of boyish-looking.

BARON It's the way she does her hair.

IRINA *(Eyes closed)* I must find another job. I really must. I'm wilting in that place. *(Eyes open)* Remember what I used to dream of?—Work that was stimulating, fulfilling, 'creative'. And look what I've ended up with—sheer damn drudgery. *(Knocking on the floor from below)* That's the doctor. Signal back to him, Nickolay. I can't. Too tired. *(The* BARON *stamps on the floor in response.)* Now he'll be up like a light. Did you know that Andrey and himself were at the card-school in the club last night and lost again? I'm told Andrey lost 200 roubles on one hand alone. Something must be done about it.

MASHA *(Indifferently)* A bit late in the day.

IRINA He lost a lot of money two weeks ago too, and a lot of money in December. If he'd just go and gamble away everything we've got, the sooner we might escape from this place. D'you know—every night, every single night in life I dream about Moscow. My God! Sometimes I think I'm going off my head. *(Laughs)* Yes, yes, I *know* we're moving there in June. But it's—what?—February, March, April, May—it's almost six months till June!

MASHA The main thing is that Natasha doesn't find out about his gambling.

IRINA Of course she knows. Does she care any more?

CHEBUTYKIN *enters the diningroom. He has been sleeping. He combs his beard, sits at the table, and begins reading a paper.*

MASHA The Little Emperor! Has he paid any rent since?

IRINA *(Laughs)* Since what? Not a halfpenny in ages! It must just never occur to him.

MASHA *laughs with her.*

MASHA And would you look at him—like a little bantam rooster.

All three laugh except VERSHININ.

IRINA You're very quiet.

VERSHININ Me? Am I? I've had nothing to eat since breakfast.

MASHA He's dying for a cup of tea.

VERSHININ My right arm for a cup of tea!

CHEBUTYKIN Irina!

IRINA Hello.

CHEBUTYKIN Have you a moment? Venez ici.

IRINA Vengo subito—isn't that right?

She goes and sits at the table with him.

CHEBUTYKIN What would I do without you?

She lays out the cards for patience. Silence.

VERSHININ Well, since nobody's going to bring us tea, can't we at least talk?

BARON *(With excessive enthusiasm)* Excellent idea! What will our topic be, Colonel?

VERSHININ Topic? Oh . . . let's . . . just . . . chat.

BARON Chat? Splendid! What will we chat about?

VERSHININ Let's try to imagine what life will be like long after we're dead and gone—say in two or three hundred years time.

BARON Good! So we're dead and buried? Excellent! Firstly people will glide across the great blue sky in enormous balloons. *(Response from* IRINA.*)* Secondly there will be totally new styles in men's jackets. *(*MASHA *and* VERSHININ *exchange looks; suppressed smiles.)* Thirdly it is conceivable that a sixth sense may be discovered and—and—and developed, to coin a phrase. *But:* and this is really the core of my thesis, life will be essentially the same. Oh, yes. Life will still be as difficult and as mysterious and as joyous and as exuberant as it is now. I promise you. And in a thousand years from now you'll still have people whining about how 'dreary' their life is. But those self-same whiners will still be as unwilling to die and as scared of dying as we are. Would you agree, Colonel?

VERSHININ I suppose so . . . Yes, of course there'll be change—that's inevitable. But in two or three hundred years time, in a thousand years time—and in a way time hasn't much to do with it—I think, yes, I'm convinced that a new kind of life, a truly happy life, will have evolved. We won't experience it, of course. But our lives here, now—our work, our anxieties, our sufferings—that's all a kind of preparation, almost a process of distillation. That's the purpose of our existence. And because it is our purpose, it is the only possibility of happiness we have.

47

MASHA *laughs quietly.*

BARON   What are you laughing at, Masha?

MASHA   I don't know. Sorry. I've been laughing all day.

VERSHININ   I went to the same cadet school as you did but I never made it to staff college; so that even though I read a lot, I was never a discriminating reader. I probably read all the wrong things. But the longer I live, the more I want to know. I'm going grey; I'm getting old; and I know so little. But there is one thing I do know, one truth I'm convinced of, and I want to convince you of it ——

BARON   Convince me!

VERSHININ   *(With passion)* We're never going to know happiness in our time. And we mustn't expect it. Because we have no right to it. Our fate is to work and work and work. Happiness isn't for us. It's for our descendants. I'll never experience it. Neither will you. But there is a possibility that my children's children may. *(His dismissive gesture)* Well . . .

FEDOTIK *and* RODDEY *enter the diningroom and sit at the end of the table.* RODDEY *plays the guitar—* Won't You Buy My Pretty Flowers?—*and hums softly.*

BARON   If I understand you correctly the point you're trying to make is this: even to dream of happiness is futile. *But:* supposing I say to you, as indeed I do, 'I am happy now'.

VERSHININ   *(Casually, dismissively)* You're not.

TUSENBACH *claps his hands and laughs loudly.*

BARON   Just like that! But I am! I am! How do you communicate with a man like that!

MASHA *laughs quietly, privately.*

BARON   Masha, I wish you'd either share your joke with us or else ——

MASHA   Sorry—sorry.

BARON   No, no, life does not change. It follows its own

inevitable laws that are outside us and beyond our understanding. Two hundred years, three hundred years, a million years, any length you want, everything will be the same. Look at the birds. Look at the cranes that head south every winter. Do they choose to migrate? Do they understand why they migrate? Not at all! They just fly south instinctively. And if there is a silly thought in their heads when they're flying, even a profound thought, does that matter? Let them philosophise as much as they like as long as they keep on flying. And I promise you, they will.

MASHA So the whole thing has no meaning?

BARON Meaning? It's snowing out there. What's the 'meaning' of that?

MASHA I think we must have a faith, and if we haven't we must find one. Because if we don't, life is empty and senseless. We must have some explanation why cranes fly south, why children are born, why there are stars in the sky. Some system of belief. Because either you know what you are living for or else nothing matters—the whole thing is absurd.

VERSHININ *has been gazing at her throughout her speech.*

VERSHININ I know just one thing.

MASHA What's that?

VERSHININ That I'm not a young man any more.

She laughs, goes to him, and catches his arm reassuringly.

MASHA What's that line from Gogol? 'Life on earth is a complete bore, my friends'—*(Softly)* to coin a phrase.

They laugh quietly, privately.

BARON And arguing with you two is impossible, my friends. 'Faith'! For God's sake!

CHEBUTYKIN *(Reads)* 'Balzac was married in Berdichev town.' Must make a note of that. *(As before he produces his pencil and notebook but puts them away almost immediately.)* What am I writing that nonsense for? Rubbish-rubbish-rubbish.

ANFISA   IRINA *picks up the line and dreamily sings a polka-style melody.*

IRINA   *(Sings)* 'Balzac was married in Berdichev town.'

RODDY *picks up the melody and plays the line once on his guitar.* IRINA *leaves down the cards and sings the line again.*

IRINA   'Balzac was married in Berdichev town.'

IRINA *and* FEDOTIK *now sing together to Roddey's accompaniment.*

BOTH   'Balzac was married in Berdichev town.'
FEDOTIK   *(Without breaking the rhythm)* Who to?
IRINA   *(Sings)* 'To a Polish girl called Hanska.'

Pause. There is a sense that this moment could blossom, an expectancy that suddenly everybody might join in the chorus—and dance—and that the room might be quickened with music and laughter. Everyone is alert to this expectation; it is almost palpable, if some means of realising it could be found. VERSHININ *moves close to* MASHA. *If the moment blossoms, they will certainly dance.* FEDOTIK *moves close to* IRINA *(to Roddey's acute annoyance); they, too, will dance.* TUSENBACH *sits at the piano. As soon as he begins picking out the melody*

FEDOTIK   Good man, Baron!

And to encourage him IRINA *and* FEDOTIK *sing the first two lines again to Roddey's accompaniment. The* BARON *is all thumbs—the melody is drowned.*

BARON   I'm lost. I need music. I can't play without music.

He shrugs his shoulders and rises from the piano.
The moment is lost. IRINA *picks up the cards.*
MASHA *drifts away from* VERSHININ. FEDOTIK *moves*
away from IRINA *and goes back to* RODDEY. *There*
is an atmosphere of vague embarrassment. And
RODDEY *now picks out the melody at an ironic,*
funereal pace.

BARON I forgot to tell you: I've taken the plunge; I've resigned my commission!

> *This evokes no response whatever.* TUSENBACH
> *waits. Silence.*

BARON What d'you make of that, Masha?
MASHA Sorry?
BARON I'm leaving the army!
MASHA *(Vaguely)* Oh? . . . yes, yes, that's good . . .
BARON So?
MASHA So what?
BARON So I'm practically a civilian!
MASHA I prefer military men.
BARON Do you? Ah . . .

> RODDY *strikes one deep quivering note on his*
> *guitar.*

BARON The only people who get quick promotion in the army these days are the pretty boys. That rules me out. Not that that worries me.

> RODDEY *strikes one high, mocking note.*

BARON I'm going to get a real job, and I'm going to work so hard—maybe it'll be for only one day in my life—but for that one day I'm going to work so hard that when I come home in the evening I'll collapse exhausted into bed and fall asleep instantly. The only people who sleep really soundly are labourers—unskilled labourers.

> *And as he goes up to the diningroom* RODDEY
> *plays a final cadence—an amen cadence—on his*
> *guitar.*

51

FEDOTIK *(To* IRINA*)* I got you these colouring crayons in that new toy shop in Moscow Street.

IRINA Why do you treat me as if I were a child?

FEDOTIK And this pen-knife.

IRINA I'm a young woman and you must—*(She breaks off, her face lighting up with childish pleasure at the crayons.)* Oh, they're lovely, they're really lovely!

FEDOTIK And wait till you see: I got this knife for myself. What about that! *(Their heads together like two children as they examine the toys. Demonstrating)* One blade. Two blades. Three blades. Four blades!

IRINA And a nail-file!

FEDOTIK Voilà—a pair of miniature scissors!

IRINA And a thing for taking stones out of horses' hooves!

FEDOTIK A miniature miracle, isn't it?

IRINA 'Miniature miracle'!

They laugh together.

RODDEY *(Irritable with jealousy)* Doctor!

CHEBUTYKIN Yes?

RODDEY Do *you* still play children's games? What age are you?

CHEBUTYKIN Me? I'm thirty-two.

Laughter at this. FEDOTIK *and* RODDEY *stare angrily at one another. Then* FEDOTIK *turns to* IRINA.

FEDOTIK I've had to learn another kind of patience. Let me show it to you.

He sits beside IRINA *at the table, and immediately* RODDEY *sings raucously and in parody.*

RODDEY 'Balzac was married in Berdichev town . . .' *(To the end.)*

As he sings ANFISA *carries in the samovar and* NATASHA *brings two plates of food.* SOLYONY *enters.*

SOLYONY Evening. Evening. Evening.

As he passes the BARON *he mimes his quack-quack and goes to the table.*

VERSHININ   There's a wind getting up.

MASHA   I'm sick of winter. Sick of it. I've forgotten what summer feels like.

IRINA   It's working out! Look—it is! It's an omen! That means we *will* go to Moscow.

FEDOTIK   No, it's not working out. That eight shouldn't be on top of the two of spades. So you won't go to Moscow.

CHEBUTYKIN   *(Reads)* 'The local outbreak of smallpox is of epidemic proportions.' *(Mock horror.)* We'll all be smit!

ANFISA   *(Coming down to* MASHA*)* Masha, the tea's poured, love. *(To* VERSHININ*)* Sorry I'm so slow, Sir— Colonel—Your Honour—if you'd come up here— I beg your pardon—what's this your name is again?

VERSHININ   It's ——

MASHA   Bring it down here, Nanny.

ANFISA   But it's all ——

MASHA   I'm not going in there.

IRINA   Nanny!

ANFISA   'Nanny! Nanny!' Coming-coming-coming!

NATASHA *hands tea to* SOLYONY *who is sprinkling his hands with perfume.*

NATASHA   They understand everything, you know. 'Morning, Bobik', I said. 'Morning, my darling little gosling.'

SOLYONY   'Gosling'?

And he looks quickly across at the BARON *and gives his quack-quack mime.*

NATASHA   And d'you know what he did?

SOLYONY   *(With exaggerated interest)* What did he do?

NATASHA   He gave me this—you know—this highly intellectual look, you know? True as God it was uncanny! And now you're thinking that's just a silly, doting mammy talking. But that's where you're wrong. You see our Bobik? I'm telling you, Captain: the stuff of genius.

SOLYONY I can imagine.

NATASHA I know it here *(her heart)*. Mammies know these things.

SOLYONY In that case, and if he were my child, d'you know what I'd do?

NATASHA What?

SOLYONY I'd fillet him, roast him and eat him. Bobik stroganoff!

And immediately he lifts his glass and comes down to the drawingroom.

NATASHA God but it's easy seen you've never had no manners nor breeding, you pup you!

MASHA If you were happy you wouldn't notice whether it's summer or winter. If I were in Moscow I wouldn't give a damn what the weather was like. At least I think I wouldn't.

VERSHININ I've just been reading the diary of a French cabinet minister that he wrote in jail—he was sentenced over the Panama Canal swindle. And he writes with such enthusiasm about the birds he sees from his cell window—birds he'd never even noticed when he was in government. And now he's out of jail he pays no more attention to the birds than he did before. Like you and Moscow: once you're living there, it'll mean nothing to you. Happiness? I don't believe in it. I don't believe it exists. Happiness is . . . a mirage.

ANFISA *hands him a cup of tea and a letter.*

ANFISA A letter for you, Sir.

VERSHININ For me?

TUSENBACH *picks up the chocolate box from the table.*

BARON What happened the chocolates?

IRINA Solyony ate them.

BARON The whole box?

He looks at SOLYONY. SOLYONY *mimes his quack-quack at him.*

54

VERSHININ	*(To* MASHA*)* From my daughter. One line on a jotter page.
MASHA	Is something wrong?
VERSHININ	I've got to go, Masha. I'm sorry. I won't have tea.
MASHA	What is it?
VERSHININ	Another crisis.
MASHA	Can't you tell me? Is it private?
VERSHININ	My wife—she's taken an overdose again. I must go. I'll just slip out quietly. It's all so . . . grotesque, isn't it? *(He kisses her hand.)* My darling—my wonderful, marvellous darling. I'll leave by the back stairs. Nobody'll notice. *(He leaves.)*
ANFISA	Where's *he* away to? Haven't I just poured him his tea! What sort of a quare buck's that?
MASHA	*(Angrily)* Shut up, will you! You keep nagging, nagging, nagging! Leave me alone, will you! I'm sick, sick, sick of your damned nagging, you old . . . nuisance!

She goes up to the diningroom with her cup.

ANFISA	Did I do something wrong, darling?
ANDREY	*(Off)* Anfisa! Anfisa!
ANFISA	'Anfisa! Anfisa!' He sits in there all day and expects everyone to ——

She is too exasperated to finish. She goes off.
MASHA *is now at the diningroom table.*

MASHA	And where am I supposed to sit? *(She sweeps the cards aside.)* Must the whole table be covered with cards?
IRINA	Masha!

Everyone is now staring at MASHA. *She stares defiantly back.*

MASHA	Haven't you all got tea to drink?
IRINA	God but you're cranky.
MASHA	If I'm cranky, don't talk to me then. Just leave me alone.
CHEBUTYKIN	*(Laughing)* Don't touch her! Careful! Don't touch her!

MASHA Look at him, would you—sixty if he's a day—and still blathering like a bloody child!

NATASHA Masha, please! Must you use coarse language like that? A girl like you, too, who could have entré into the very best society. But I mean to say, dear, when you have recourse to vernacular vulgarities— tch-tch-tch, oh my goodness! Je vous prie, pardonnez-moi, mais vous avez des manières peu grossières.

The situation is defused. TUSENBACH *can scarcely suppress his laughter.*

BARON Could I have some —— Isn't there brandy somewhere? Where's the brandy gone?

NATASHA Il paraît que mon Bobik déjà ne dort pas—the little darling's awake. Better see how he is. He's out of sorts today. If you'll excuse me . . .

She leaves.

IRINA *(To* MASHA*)* Where's the colonel?

MASHA Gone.

IRINA Gone where?

MASHA Home. 'Home'! His wife's done something . . . theatrical again.

TUSENBACH, *already slightly intoxicated, goes with the bottle of brandy to* SOLYONY *who is sitting apart as usual.*

BARON You're always sitting by yourself, brooding about something or other, God alone knows what. Come on, Solyony, let's make it up, let's have a brandy together. *(They drink.)* A little refreshment before the mummers arrive 'cos then I'll be stuck at the piano all night. But what the bloody hell—to use a vernacular vulgarity.

SOLYONY I've never quarrelled with you. What have we to make up?

BARON Just that I always have the feeling that there's some —some tension between us; that's all. I'll tell you what you are, Solyony.

SOLYONY   Here we go.

BARON   You are what Kulygin would call a rara avis—that is to say, a rare bird.

SOLYONY   'I may be odd, but who is not; Aleko, be not angry.'

While they are talking ANDREY *enters with his book and sits at the table.*

BARON   Aleko who? What are you talking about?

SOLYONY   When I'm alone with somebody I'm perfectly relaxed, at ease, normal. It's only when I'm in company that I become difficult, aggressive.

FEDOTIK *comes down beside them, picks up the brandy bottle, looks at it, leaves it down again.*

FEDOTIK   Sorry. Thought it was vodka.

He moves away.

SOLYONY   At the same time I'm a lot more honest, a lot less queer, than some people I could name.

BARON   And I'll be honest with you, Solyony. I do get angry with you—yes—especially when there are people about and you deliberately set out to bait me. *But:* I like you—yes, I like you—yes, I like Solyony. Oh, what the hell—I'm going to get loaded tonight. Let's get loaded together.

SOLYONY   Why not. *(They drink.)* No, I've nothing against you, Baron. It's just that I'm a Lermontov type.

BARON   A what type?

SOLYONY   You know the writer, Lermontov.

BARON   Know the name.

SOLYONY   I've his temperament—disenchanted, bored, caustic.

BARON   Good Lord!

SOLYONY   *(Quietly, confidentially)* I've even been told I resemble him physically, too. Strange that, isn't it?

He perfumes his hands.

BARON   It's all over, Solyony: I've resigned my commission.

57

Thought about it for five years and now it's done.
Now I'm going to get a real job, a man's job.

SOLYONY To coin a phrase.

BARON Ha-ha. To coin a phrase. Very good. Very good. Who says that?

SOLYONY 'Aleko, be not angry;
Forget, forget your dreams.'

BARON Aleko, my friend, from now on it's going to be all work, work, work.

CHEBUTYKIN *comes down to the drawingroom with* IRINA.

CHEBUTYKIN I was there for only one night but the meat they gave us was genuine Caucasian food: vegetable soup followed by chemartma. That's a kind of meat dish.

SOLYONY Onion.

CHEBUTYKIN What's that?

SOLYONY Cheremsha's not meat. Cheremsha's a kind of onion.

CHEBUTYKIN Who mentioned cheremsha?

SOLYONY Bit like a shallot.

CHEBUTYKIN I'm talking about a mutton dish called chemartma.

SOLYONY Cheremsha's not mutton.

CHEBUTYKIN But chemartma *is* mutton.

SOLYONY Cheremsha's made from onions.

CHEBUTYKIN Who's arguing with you? We're talking about two different dishes, Solyony. Anyhow you've never been to the Caucasus. Or eaten chemartma.

SOLYONY Because I can't stand the smell of it. Cheremsha stinks, just like garlic.

ANDREY For God's sake will you two please stop!

BARON I want the mummers! Bring on the dancing mummers!

IRINA They promised they'd be here about nine. They should be here any time now.

TUSENBACH *goes unsteadily to* ANDREY *and embraces him.*

BARON *(Sings)* 'There are many sad and weary ——'

ANDREY *(Sings)* '—— in this pleasant world of ours.'

TOGETHER	'Crying every night so dreary' Won't you buy my pretty flowers?'

They laugh raucously and TUSENBACH *kisses* ANDREY.

BARON	Bloody hell—let's have one modest little drink. *(Toast.)* To my eternal friendship with my friend, Andrey Prozorov. And when Andrey Prozorov goes back to Moscow University, his eternal friend goes, too.
SOLYONY	Goes where?
BARON	To Moscow University.
SOLYONY	Which one?
BARON	'Which one'! There is but one Moscow University.
SOLYONY	Two universities in Moscow.
BARON	One.
SOLYONY	Two.
BARON	One.
ANDREY	Who cares if there's a hundred. The more the merrier.
SOLYONY	There are two universities in Moscow.

Good humoured booing and hissing and cries of 'Shut up, Solyony!'

SOLYONY	In Moscow there are two universities. *(Louder protests.* SOLYONY *now has to shout to be heard.)* But if you find what I have to say too disagreeable and if you find me too unpleasant, I can always go somewhere else, can't I?

He leaves.

BARON	You can. And good riddance, too. *(Laughs.)* Everybody on the floor, my friends. Music will be provided by Baron Tusenbach and His Tigers. A rara avis, Solyony. But ignore him—ignore him.

He sits at the piano and thumps out The Blue Danube Waltz. MASHA *dances by herself. As before there is the possibility that the occasion might blossom. But there is less possibility this time.*

MASHA   *(Sings)* 'The baron is drunk, is drunk, is drunk;
            The baron is drunk, is drunk, is drunk . . .'

While she sings NATASHA *enters.*

NATASHA   Where's the doctor?
CHEBUTYKIN Hello!

NATASHA *passes* MASHA *to go to the doctor and,
as she passes,* MASHA *sings directly to her*

MASHA   'The baron is pissed, is pissed, is pissed;
            I wished I were pissed, full pissed, mad pissed.
            Was she ever pissed, full pissed, half-pissed? . . .'

NATASHA *has whispered into the doctor's ear and
now leaves.* CHEBUTYKIN *goes to the piano and
whispers to the* BARON. *The* BARON *stops playing.
Silence—apart from Masha's singing and she
persists.*

MASHA   'Ta-ra-ra-ra-ra, ta-ra, ta-ra;
            Ta-ra-ra-ra-ra . . .'

Now she fades out.

IRINA   *(To* CHEBUTYKIN*)* What's the matter?
CHEBUTYKIN Time we were going. Good night.
BARON   Good night, everybody. Time to pack up.
IRINA   Wait a minute! What about the mummers?
ANDREY   The mummers aren't coming! *(Now very embar-
rassed)* What has happened is that . . . the position
is that Bobik . . . Bobik's not too well according to
his mother . . . and . . . and . . . that's that. That's
all I know. Nothing more. Just what I'm told.

He exits quickly. CHEBUTYKIN *follows him.*

IRINA   *(Shrugs)* If Bobik's not too well . . .
MASHA   What the hell. If we're being evicted *(Shouts)* then
we ought to leave quietly, mustn't we? *(To* IRINA*)*
Nothing the matter with Bobik. It's mammy who's
—*(she taps her head)*—just a little bit. *(Loudly)*
Bitch!

FEDOTIK Too bad, isn't it. And I was looking forward to a good night. But of course if the baby's sick ... I'll get him some toys tomorrow. 'Bye.

RODDEY Oh, my! Such a disappointment, my petals. And you'd never guess what I did this afternoon immediately after lunch—went to bed for an hour so that I'd be in positively dazzling form this evening! I mean I thought we'd be dancing all night, didn't I? My goodness me, we can't let the night end like this, my petals—can we? It's only nine o'clock! The day's only beginning!

MASHA We'll go outside. We'll decide then what do do.

They all leave. Voices off calling 'Good night—good night'. *The* BARON *sings* 'The baron is drunk, is drunk, is drunk' *and laughs drunkenly. Gradually the sounds fade.* ANFISA *and a maid enter, clear the table, put out the lights. Off stage a nurse sings to the baby.* ANDREY *and* CHEBUTYKIN *enter, preparing to go out.*

CHEBUTYKIN I never got round to marrying. Somehow life went past too quickly on me. Anyhow the only woman I ever loved passionately was already married. That was your mother.

ANDREY *(Not listening)* Nobody should get married. Ever. Marriage is—is—is stultifying.

CHEBUTYKIN Maybe. But the alternative is loneliness. And loneliness can be stultifying, too, young man. Agh, what matter. Who gives a damn!

ANDREY Come on. Let's get out of here.

CHEBUTYKIN Take your time. We're too early.

ANDREY Will you move before Natasha comes in and stops me?

CHEBUTYKIN You're right.

ANDREY I'm not going to gamble tonight. I'm just going to sit and watch.

CHEBUTYKIN What's wrong?

ANDREY I don't feel so well. I get this shortness of breath. What should I take for it?

CHEBUTYKIN You're asking *me*? What are you asking me for. I wouldn't know. I don't remember.

ANDREY We'll go out through the kitchen.

They go out. The doorbell rings. ANFISA *goes to
the window and looks down. The bell rings again.
Voices and laughter off—the mummers have
arrived.* IRINA *enters.*

IRINA   Who is it, Nanny?
ANFISA   *(Whispers)* The mummers! All dressed up!
IRINA   Tell them—tell them there's no one at home. Say
you're very sorry but there's no one at home.

ANFISA *goes off.* IRINA *is alone. She walks around,
deep in thought. She is very distressed.* SOLYONY
enters.

SOLYONY   *(Astonished)* Is there nobody here? Where's every-
body gone?
IRINA   Home.
SOLYONY   Well! So you're on your own?
IRINA   Yes. *(Pause)* Goodnight, Solyony.
SOLYONY   I'm sorry. I behaved badly just now. That shouldn't
have happened. But you're not like the others,
Irina. You're away above all that kind of stupid,
stupid messing. I think you understand me. Yes, I
know you do. *(Pause)* I'm in love with you, Irina.
I love you deeply. I love you passionately.
IRINA   You'd better go. Good night, Solyony.
SOLYONY   I can't live without you. *(She moves away. He
follows.)* Just to be with you. Just to gaze at you.
Just to see those magical, amazing eyes of yours ——
IRINA   Please, Captain. Stop.
SOLYONY   The first time I've ever told you how much I love
you and, just to be able to articulate it to you, it
makes me feel . . . transformed.
IRINA   Stop it! At once!

    Pause.

SOLYONY   Of course . . . of course . . . I can't force you to
love me . . . naturally . . . But I want you to under-
stand this: I won't let anybody else have you. Let
there be no doubt about that, Irina. Because if
there is somebody else—*(Pause)*—I will kill him.

That's a promise. I will kill him. *(Again he moves towards her.)* Irina, my beautiful, beautiful Irina, please listen for a second to ——

He breaks off because NATASHA *enters, wearing her housecoat and carrying a candle. As before she opens doors, peers in, closes them again. As she passes Andrey's room she taps on the door but does not open it.*

NATASHA   It's only me, Andrey. Just checking. Don't stir Read away. *(Now she sees* SOLYONY. *Coldly)* I didn't know you were here, Captain. You'll have to excuse me. I know I'm not correctly dressed to receive guests.

SOLYONY   Who cares? Good night.

He leaves.

NATASHA   Irina, darling—*(kisses her)*—you're exhausted; I know you are. You should try to get to bed a bit earlier.

IRINA   Is Bobik asleep?

NATASHA   At last. But restless, tossing about. By the way, darling, I keep meaning to ask you but either you're out or else I'm too busy.

IRINA   Ask me what?

NATASHA   Bobik's nursery—it's so cold and so damp. But your room—it'd be just perfect for a baby. Darling, would you ever think of moving in with Olga for a while?

IRINA   *(Not understanding)* Move in where?

A troika with bells is heard drawing up outside. NATASHA *responds briefly but pursues her present task.*

NATASHA   You can share with Olga for the time being and Bobik can have your room. *(Doorbell rings.)* That'll be Olga, won't it? Isn't she late? *(Back to her task.)* That's grand. That's a weight off my mind. He's

63

such a darling. This morning I said to him, 'Morning, Bobik. Morning, my darling little gosling'. And d'you know what he did? He ——

She breaks off because a maid has entered and whispers in her ear.

NATASHA *(Sharply)* What is it? What is it? *(More whispering. Coyly)* Protopopov? Lord, isn't he a caution! *(To* IRINA*)* It's Protopopov—to invite me out for a drive in his new troika. The naughty thing! *(Laughs)* Men! You couldn't be up to them, could you! Maybe I'll go for just a little ride, a quarter of an hour or so—what d'you think? Maybe I shouldn't—should I? Sure what harm's in it. *(To maid)* Tell him I'll be down in a minute. *(Doorbell again.)* That'll be Olga now.

She goes off. Pause. Then VERSHININ, OLGA *and* KULYGIN *enter.*

KULYGIN Well-well-well—what's this? I thought you said we were going to have a party?

VERSHININ I thought so. I left only half an hour ago and they were expecting the mummers then.

IRINA Everybody's gone. Everybody's left.

KULYGIN Has Masha gone, too? Where did she go? And what's Protopopov doing out there in his troika? Who's he waiting for? And where's the baron and ——

IRINA Fyodor, please. Don't bombard me with questions. I'm tired.

KULYGIN Now-now—don't be a Little Miss Cross Patch Draw The Latch!

OLGA The staff meeting has only just finished and I'm just spent. And the headmistress is sick and I've got to take on her work. Oh my head, my head. This migraine's becoming unbearable. *(She drops into a seat.)* And the whole town's talking about Andrey: he lost two hundred roubles at cards last night.

KULYGIN Yes, that meeting was a bit testing, wasn't it? *(He sits.)*

Pause.

VERSHININ What happened was . . . my wife for some reason best known to herself, she decided to give me a fright . . . tried to poison herself . . . No harm done. Another false alarm. Everything's in hand, I think . . . So there's no party? I suppose we should go, then? *(Suddenly eager)* Kulygin, what about you and I going somewhere ourselves? Come on, man! I can't face going home yet. I really can't. What d'you say?

KULYGIN I'm too tired. Some other time. *(He stands up.)* I'm really very tired. Do you think Masha has gone home?

IRINA I suppose so.

KULYGIN Well—good night. *(Kisses Irina's hand.)* At least we have the weekend to recuperate. 'Bye. *(He moves off.)* I would have liked a refreshing cup of tea. I would have enjoyed an evening of relaxed sociability. But there you are. O fallacem hominum spem; that is to say—the false hopes that men entertain. Fallacem spem—the accusative of exclamation.

VERSHININ Looks as if I'll have to go somewhere by myself. Good night.

VERSHININ *and* KULYGIN *leave.*

OLGA This migraine's getting worse and worse . . . Did I tell you?—Andrey lost two hundred roubles; it's the talk of the town. Yes, I did tell you . . . I'm off to bed. No work tomorrow or the next day; thanks be to God for that . . . Oh my poor head . . .

She leaves. As at the opening of this Act in the far distance a girl hums Won't You Buy My Pretty Flowers? *and is accompanied by a piano accordion. The music is slow and haunting and sad.* NATASHA *enters and crosses the stage briskly. She is wearing an expensive fur coat and matching fur hat. A maid trots behind her carrying a matching fur muff.*

65

NATASHA Back in half an hour! Just going for a little drive! Au revoir!

IRINA *is alone on stage. Long silence. Then*

IRINA *(With intense longing)* Oh, Moscow! Moscow! Moscow!

QUICK BLACK. END OF ACT TWO

ACT THREE

It is almost 3.00 a.m., a mid-summer night. A year and a half has passed.

The bedroom shared by OLGA *and* IRINA. *Two beds, one stage left and one stage right, each with a screen around it. A large sofa stage left. Also a large wardrobe. A wash-hand basin and jug stage right. Above it a very large mirror. Off stage a bell is ringing (perhaps a churchbell) because fire has broken out in the town some time previously. Nobody in the house has gone to bed yet.*

MASHA, *dressed in black as usual, is lying on the sofa, her eyes closed.* OLGA *enters. She is very agitated.* ANFISA *trots exhaustedly behind her.*

ANFISA They're sitting down there now, the poor creatures, crying their eyes out. I've told them a dozen times to come upstairs, not to sit down there. But I can't get a budge out of them. 'Where's Daddy?', they're crying. 'Maybe Daddy's burned to death.' The poor wee souls. And there's a crowd outside in the yard too, with hardly a stitch on them. According to them Kirsanovsky Street's burned to the ground.

> OLGA *rapidly pulls dresses out of the wardrobe, choosing certain garments only. She flings them into Anfisa's open arms.*

OLGA Take this grey one, Nanny. And this one, too. And this blouse. And this skirt. My God, what a disaster! Here—take this—and this—and this. (ANFISA *almost staggers under the weight.)* The poor Vershinins must have got a terrible fright—their house is badly damaged. They must stay the night here; we mustn't allow them to go home. And poor Fedotik lost everything—not a single thing saved.

ANFISA You'd better call Ferapont, love. (OLGA *rings a hand bell.)* I'm not fit to carry all ——

OLGA Why doesn't he come when I ring? (*She flings open the door and calls.)* Come on, come on, Ferapont! Where are you? (*Through the open door can be seen a window red with the fire.)* Oh my God, this is terrible, terrible!

FERAPONT enters. OLGA returns to the wardrobe and now strips it indiscriminately.

OLGA   Here, man, take these downstairs. Give them to the Sakarov girls to distribute. Here; and give them this too.

FERAPONT   Did you ever hear tell, Miss, that in the year one thousand, eight hundred and twelve Moscow was burned down too—just like this. And when the French saw it hee-hee-hee they were so shocked they ——

OLGA   Will you move, man!

FERAPONT   Wha's that, Miss?

OLGA   Go! Go! Go!

FERAPONT   Yes, Miss. Certainly, Miss.

He leaves.

OLGA   Give them everything we have, Nanny, everything. *(She empties what is left in the wardrobe on to the bed.)* What do we need it for? Give it all away—everything—everything—everything . . .

The wardrobe is now empty. OLGA is suddenly exhausted. She sits on the bed. Rises immediately.

OLGA   No, we must keep going. Now. The Vershinins will stay the night. The two little girls can sleep in the drawingroom and their father can go in with Baron Tusenbach in the back bedroom. Fedotik can sleep there too—or in the diningroom, if he wants. We can put no one in with the doctor. I'm so angry with him. What sort of a man deliberately goes and gets drunk on a night like this! Who else is there? Yes—Vershinin's wife. She'd better go into the drawingroom too, with her two little girls.

ANFISA   *(Exhausted, speaking softly)* Don't send me away, Miss Olga. Please don't send me away.

OLGA   Away where? What are you talking about, Nanny? *(She goes to her.)* Who's sending you away? What sort of silly talk is that?

She sits beside ANFISA *who puts her head on Olga's shoulder.*

ANFISA   I work as hard as I can, love. Honest to God I do. But the moment I'm not fit to carry on, I'll be told to go. And sure I've nowhere to go to, Olga—you know that. I'm eighty, love, amn't I? No. I must be well over eighty. I must be eighty-one or eighty-two or ——

OLGA   Shhhhhhhh, Nanny darling, shush-shush-shush. You're worn out tonight, that's all. You're just exhausted. So just sit here and rest for a while. Shhhhhh . . .

And she rocks ANFISA *in her arms for a few seconds.* NATASHA *enters. She moves around the room as she talks, mentally noting the clothes on the floor, the empty wardrobe, etc.*

NATASHA   They're talking about setting up a relief committee for the families that have lost their homes. I'm all for that. One must always be ready to help the underprivileged. Shouldn't one? *(She studies herself in the mirror.)* I mean to say, if the privileged classes don't undertake their civic responsibilities, I mean to say, who will? They're fast asleep, the wee darlings—Bobik and wee Sophie—dead to the world as if nothing had happened. If you'd seen the crowd there is downstairs—God bless us and save us!—like the harvest fair day! And there's a bad 'flu going about. I hope the wee ones don't get it.

OLGA   It's so peaceful in this room. You wouldn't know there was a fire at all.

NATASHA   Sweet mother of God, would you look at that hair! D'you think I've put on weight? Maybe a bit. Some people tell me I'm not near as soigné as I was before wee Sophie was born. What d'you think? *(She turns round.)* Ah! Poor Masha's asleep, the creature. Exhausted, the soul. And sure aren't we all?

Now for the first time she sees ANFISA. *Her fury is instant and excessive, almost hysterical.*

69

NATASHA   You! How dare you sit in my presence! *(*ANFISA *rises quickly. So does* OLGA.*)* Get up and get out! Out! Out! Out!

ANFISA *leaves.*

NATASHA   I'll never understand why you keep that old woman about the place!

OLGA   And, if you'll forgive me, I don't understand how ——

NATASHA   She's no use any more! She's a peasant and that's where she belongs—out in the bogs! You have her spoiled! If this house is ever to be run properly, we cannot carry old baggage like that.

OLGA *sits.* NATASHA *is suddenly calm again. She strokes Olga's cheek.*

NATASHA   Ah, poor Olga's tired. Our headmistress is tired. Do you realise that when wee Sophie grows up and goes to grammar school I'll be scared of you?

OLGA   I won't be headmistress.

NATASHA   Oh but you will, darling. That's all been arranged.

OLGA   I'll turn it down. I couldn't do it. I could never handle it. *(She takes a drink of water.)* You were very rude to Nanny just now, Natasha. And I hope I'm not offending you but I just cannot endure that sort of behaviour; it makes me feel . . . weak.

NATASHA   I'm sorry, Olga. Honest to God I'm sorry. Sure I wouldn't upset you for all the tea in China.

MASHA *stands up, takes her pillow, and exits angrily.*

OLGA   What I'm trying to say is that—that—maybe the way we were brought up seems peculiar to you. But to hear a servant talked to like that upsets me terribly. I just can't—it just makes me feel actually . . . physically sick.

NATASHA   *(Kissing her)* I'm sorry—I'm sorry—I'm sorry—I'm sorry ——

OLGA	Even a rude word—whatever silly way I'm made—even a tactless word ——
NATASHA	And sure nobody's more tactless than I am. I know. I know. I'm as thick as poundies—I know that. At the same time, darling, at her time of day she'd be happier in the country somewhere—now wouldn't she?
OLGA	She's been with our family for thirty years, Natasha.
NATASHA	*(Softly, reasonably)* But she can't work any more, can she? Either I don't understand you or you don't want to understand me. *She is not able to work.* Is that not right? All she does is sleep or sit about.
OLGA	Then let her sit about!
NATASHA	Let her sit about! Sweet mother of God! She's a servant, isn't she? *(Crying)* I just don't understand you, Olga. I have a nanny for Bobik and a wet nurse for wee Sophie and we share a maid and a cook. Now: what do you keep that old bag for? Just tell me—what in God's name *for*?

The fire bell rings in the distance.

OLGA	I feel I have aged ten years this night.
NATASHA	We must come to an understanding, Olga, you and I. Your place is in the school. Mine is in the home. You teach your classes. I run this house. And when I make a decision about the servants that decision will be respected. Is that clearly understood? I do know what I'm talking about. All right. So: that old hag, that thieving old bitch clears out of this house tomorrow. *(Suddenly almost hysterical again)* And don't you ever cross me again! D'you hear me? Ever—ever—ever! *(As suddenly in control again)* God bless us and save us, if you don't leave, we'll end up having a wee tiff; and that would be awful, wouldn't it? You and me fighting—Lord, we could never have that!

KULYGIN *enters.*

KULYGIN	Is Masha not here? It's time we went home. I'm told the fire's under control now. *(He stretches*

himself) Only one street of houses was burned down despite that wind. At one point it looked as if the whole town was going to go up. *(Sits)* I *am* tired. I'll tell you something, Olga: if I hadn't married Masha, I'd have married you. Yes. You are such a *femina benevola*—that is to say, such a considerate woman. Oh, I really am tired. Shhh. *(Listens)* The doctor has to pick a night like this to go on the hammer. Footless! *(Rises)* I think he's coming up here. Yes, that's him. *(Laughs)* What a man! I'm getting out of the way.

He goes behind one of the screens.

OLGA   He doesn't touch a drop for years, and then on the one night—the only night—when he could be of some use ——

She moves up to the back of the bedroom where NATASHA *is doing her hair before a small mirror.* CHEBUTYKIN, *walking very erect, enters. He looks round the room, sees nobody. He goes to the wash-hand basin and begins washing his hands.*

CHEBUTYKIN   To hell with them. To hell with the whole lot of them. Just because I'm called 'doctor' they think I can make them all . . . whole! Me! Who knows sweet damn all! Even the sweet damn all I used to know, that's forgotten too. All gone—gone—gone.

OLGA and NATASHA slip out unnoticed.

CHEBUTYKIN   So to hell with them. *(To his reflection)* And to hell with you specifically, my friend. You know why you're drunk, don't you? Course you do. We both know. Shhhh. Last Wednesday—correct? That woman that came to see you and you diagnosed appendicitis—correct? *(Shakes his head very slowly.)* No, no, not correct at all, my friend. Because your diagnosis was incorrect and the lady died, my friend. You killed her. *(He splashes water on his face.)* Twenty-five years ago I used to know one or two things; but they're vanished too—all gone, gone,

gone . . . *(He touches his reflection with his finger tip.)* Maybe you're the reality. Why not? Maybe this *(body)* is the image. Maybe this hasn't arms and legs and a head at all. Maybe this has no existence . . . just pretends to exist . . . just pretends to walk about and eat and sleep . . . I wish that were true. I wish you *(reflection)* were the reality, my friend. I wish—oh, God, how I wish this *(body)* didn't exist . . . *(He cries. Then suddenly)* What the hell do I care? That conversation in the club the other day—*(to mirror)*—remember? Eh-eh-eh? All about Shakespeare and Voltaire. I know you— you've never read Shakespeare or Voltaire—not a line. Neither had the others. But you all pretended you were experts, didn't you? Experts? Hah! Shysters! Shabby, grubby shysters! And then suddenly you remembered the woman you had killed, all that came back to you then, expert doctor, didn't it? And suddenly you knew what you were— nothing, nothing, nothing. And splendid nothing that you are, what did you do? Went out and got loaded! Oh you are . . . magnificent.

IRINA, VERSHININ *and* TUSENBACH *enter.* VERSHININ *is dishevelled and dirty with the fire. The* BARON *is immaculate in a stylish new civilian suit.*

IRINA   Come in here and sit down. It's quieter here.
VERSHININ   Only for the soldiers the whole town would have been burned down. They were wonderful. I was really proud of them. They were . . . magnificent.

KULYGIN *emerges from behind the screen. He is winding his watch.*

KULYGIN   Has anybody got the correct time?
BARON   Ten past three. It'll soon be dawn.
IRINA   Everybody's just sitting down there in the drawing-room. Nobody seems to want to move. *(To* TUSENBACH*)* Your friend, Solyony, is down there too. Doctor, don't you think you should go to bed?
CHEBUTYKIN   I'm perfectly all right, thank you very much indeed.
KULYGIN   You naughty boy, you're inebriated, doctor!—

73

'Correct'? *(He slaps him on the back.)* In vino veritas—'Correct'?

BARON   Everybody's on to me to get up a benefit concert for the fire victims.

IRINA   And who would you get to perform in a town like this?

BARON   Oh, we could do it if we wanted to. Masha could play the piano. In my opinion Masha is a beautiful pianist.

KULYGIN   Masha? Indeed she is. Splendid.

IRINA   She used to be. She's forgotten it all now. She hasn't touched a piano for three or four years.

BARON   The trouble is, nobody in this town appreciates good music—apart from myself, if you don't mind me saying so. And I can assure you, Masha plays magnificently, almost with genius.

KULYGIN   Absolutely right, Baron. I'm very fond of Masha. Masha is a wonderful human being.

BARON   Can you imagine what it's like to be able to play so magnificently and to know that nobody, nobody . . . appreciates you, to coin a phrase?

KULYGIN   *(Sighs)* Difficult, indeed. But there is a slight problem and it's this: would it be—you know—would it be perhaps infra dignitatem for the wife of a schoolmaster to play in a concert? Maybe not. How would I know? I'm sure it would be perfectly proper. And our headmaster is a fine man, an understanding man, a highly intelligent man. But, having said all that, he does have certain inflexible attitudes. Not that this would have anything to do with him. All the same perhaps I should have a word with him . . . if you like.

CHEBUTYKIN *picks up a china clock and examines it.*

VERSHININ   That fire has me ruined. I must go and change. *(Pause)* There was a rumour going about yesterday that our brigade may be transferred. Poland was mentioned. And Siberia. You may be sure—somewhere in the back of beyond.

BARON   I heard that rumour too. Thank God I'm finished with all that. Well, when you people leave, this will be a real ghost-town!

IRINA   We're going away too.

CHEBUTYKIN drops the clock which smashes into pieces.

CHEBUTYKIN   Smashed to smithereens!

There is a very brief, shocked silence. KULYGIN moves first. He gets down on his hands and knees and begins to pick up the pieces.

KULYGIN   Oh, Doctor, Doctor, Doctor—a valuable piece like that! Oh my, oh my, oh my! Oh, a black mark, Doctor! Definitely a black mark for that!

IRINA   That was mother's clock.

CHEBUTYKIN   *(Quickly, angrily)* Don't I know that! *(Controlled)* Maybe it was, maybe it wasn't. Maybe it's not smashed. Maybe it only seems to be smashed. Maybe we don't exist. Maybe we're not here at all. *(Leaving)* Sweet damn all I know. Sweet damn all anybody knows. *(Stops at door)* What are you all staring at me for? Natasha's having an affair with Protopopov—stare at that for a change! But you'd rather not, wouldn't you? You'd rather sit with your eyes closed while Natasha and Protopopov are carrying on in front of your very noses! Hah! *(Sings)* 'There was I, waiting at the church, waiting at the church, waiting at the church ——' *(He breaks off, stares briefly at them and leaves.)*

VERSHININ   *(Speaks)* 'Waiting at the church!' *(Shakes his head slowly.)* It has been such a strange day . . . As soon as the fire started I ran home as fast as I could. When I got near the house I could see that it wasn't in danger. And my two little girls were standing at the front door in their pyjamas. No sign of their mother. People charging about, shouting, screaming —horses, dogs going mad—it was all so . . . If you'd seen the look on the children's faces: a mixture of terror and horror and entreaty. That was more terrifying than all the horrors around me. And I thought: my God, I thought, how much more have these children to go through in the years ahead. I grabbed them and ran back here with them

75

and all the time I was running I could think only one thing: how much more they will have to go through in this world. *(Fire alarm off.)* When I got here, my wife was here already . . . in some private tantrum of her own . . .

MASHA *enters with her pillow and sits on the sofa.*

VERSHININ   Telling them about seeing my two little girls standing at the front door in their pyjamas and the street in flames and everybody panicking. Like a scene from years and years ago when armies used to make sudden raids on towns and burn them and plunder them. And it struck me how different those days are to our time now. And things will get better still. Before very long—in two or three hundred years time—people will look back on our way of life the way we look back on those old days, with surprise and an element of horror; because they'll regard our way of life as—what's that quotation?—'nasty, brutish and short'. Oh yes, life is going to get better and better and better and better! *(He laughs and spreads his hands.)* Well . . . Vershinin, your instant philosopher—*(looking at the* BARON *and* KULYGIN *who are both asleep)*—guaranteed to electrify. *(Laughs)* And now that I'm in full flight, may I go on? Actually I'm in deadly earnest—not that that makes any difference. *(Softly to* MASHA *who is hugging her pillow, her eyes closed.)* How are you? You're not asleep, are you? *(She shakes her head.)* So. Where were we? Yes—great, great times ahead. *(To* IRINA*)* Today there are only three people like you in the whole of this town. But in the generations to come there will be more and more and more. And a time will arrive when things will have changed so radically that your life-style will be the norm. And when that happens, then even your enlightened attitudes will become outmoded and an even more enlightened generation will emerge. Hurrah! *(Laughs)* The gospel according to Vershinin! *(Laughs)* I want to desperately, so desperately to live . . .

	(Sings) 'We yield to love at every age And fruitful are its pains' (Laughs).
MASHA	(Eyes still closed) Ta-ra-ra-ra.
VERSHININ	(Delighted) Ta-ra.
MASHA	Ta-ra-ra-ra.
VERSHININ	Ta-ra. (And again he laughs)

FEDOTIK enters.

FEDOTIK	(Dancing) Burned to a cinder! Burned to ashes! Not a single thing left. (Laughs)
IRINA	What's funny about that? Was nothing saved?
FEDOTIK	(Laughs) Nothing! I'm cleaned out—camera, guitar, clothes, letters, dress uniform—all up in smoke! Even a little note-book I had for you—gone!

Enter SOLYONY.

IRINA	No, no, Captain. Please go away. You can't come in here.
SOLYONY	Why not?
IRINA	Please.
SOLYONY	The baron's allowed in. Why amn't I?
VERSHININ	It's time we were all going. What's the news of the fire?
SOLYONY	Dying down. (To IRINA) Well? Why do you allow the baron in and not me?

He sprinkles his hands with perfume.

VERSHININ	(Softly to MASHA) Ta-ra-ra-ra.
MASHA	(Softly to VERSHININ) Ta-ra.
VERSHININ	(Laughing, to SOLYONY) Come on, man. We'll go down to the diningroom.
SOLYONY	(To IRINA) That's all right. That's fine with me. I'll not forget this. (His icy smile) 'This issue will be made more clear; But not before the duck, my dear.'

As he passes the sleeping BARON he does his quack-quack mime into the Baron's face. Then he and VERSHININ and FEDOTIK all leave.

IRINA *(Opening a window)* Everywhere that man goes the place reeks with his damned lotions. *(She shakes* TUSENBACH.*)* Wake up. Baron. Wake up.

TUSENBACH *sits up.*

BARON What? What's the matter?

IRINA Time to go home.

BARON *(Rising and stretching)* I was dead out there. The brick-works—that's the solution.

IRINA The what?

BARON The brick-works. I've spoken to the manager. I'm to start work there first thing in the morning—one of these days. No, I'm not talking in my sleep. It's all been arranged. *(He catches her hands.)* You look so pale and so beautiful and so—so—so radiant. It's almost as if your paleness has a luminosity. Yes, yes, yes, I know how you feel; I know you're depressed; I know how unhappy you are with the way things have turned out. So I'll tell you what you'll do: we'll go away together, just the two of us; we'll go away and work together, somewhere far, far, far away.

MASHA I wish you'd just settle for home in the meantime, Nickolay.

BARON All right—all right—I'm going. *(Kissing Irina's hands)* I'm away. *(He doesn't move. He gazes at her.)* D'you remember a birthday party you had—oh, it must be four years ago now—d'you remember that party?—and you told us you had a revelation, an epiphany—d'you remember?—and you spoke about the excitement, the joy of work—d'you remember that? I remember it distinctly. I remember so clearly how happy, how vibrant you were that day. And you had so much confidence that you made everything sound so possible for all of us . . . What happened to all that? . . . All those possibilities? *(He kisses her hand again.)* Don't cry, Irina. *(Kiss)* You should be in bed. *(Kiss)* It's beginning to get light. *(Kiss)* It's almost morning. *(Kiss)* I would like to—I'd be happy to—to ——

IRINA What?

BARON *(Very simply)* I wish I could give my life for you . . .
(Now embarrassed) . . . to coin a phrase.

MASHA My God! There's caution for you! Nickolay, have you no home to go to?

BARON I'm away.

Again he kisses Irina's hand and leaves. MASHA *stretches out on the sofa and closes her eyes.*

MASHA Are you asleep, Fyodor?

KULYGIN Mmmm? What's that?

MASHA Why don't you go home?

KULYGIN My good Masha, my dear Masha, my precious Masha, I ——

IRINA She's very tired. Better let her rest, Fyodor.

KULYGIN You're right. I'll go. Masha, my love, I love you, I love only you, I love nobody but ——

MASHA *(Softly, bitterly)* Amo, amas, amat, amamus, amatis, amant.

KULYGIN *(Laughs)* Perfectly conjugated. And what does 'amamus' mean? First person plural, present tense? It means 'we love'—correct? *(To* IRINA*)* Isn't she marvellous? Seven whole years since she and I were conjugated—ha-ha, there's a splendid pun for you! —but it seems to me as if that happy occasion took place only yesterday. Honestly! *(To* MASHA*)* I mean it. You are a wonderful, wonderful human being. *(To* IRINA*)* Oh, I'm so happy, so happy, so happy.

MASHA And I'm so bored, bored, bored. *(She sits up.)* There's something I've got to tell you, something you all ought to know. I can't keep it to myself any longer. I ——

KULYGIN *(Momentary panic)* Masha, if it's something to do with you and ——

MASHA It's about Andrey. He's mortgaged this house to the bank and that wife of his has taken the money. And the point is, this house isn't his alone. It belongs to the four of us. And damn-well he knows that—if there's any decency left in him!

KULYGIN *(Relieved)* Oh, come on, Masha. Why do you want to bring that up now? You know he owes money all over the town. Poor old Andrey, he has his own bothers.

79

MASHA It's a rotten thing for him to have done! Just rotten!

She lies down again.

KULYGIN I wouldn't worry about the money. You and I are comfortably enough off, aren't we? I have my good job in the secondary school, and there's the odd private pupil, and—and—and everything's in hand, isn't it? I think so. I think so. But then I'm just your plain, average man, amn't I? Omnia mea mecum porto— that is to say, whatever I am, there it is before you.

MASHA I'm not looking for something for myself. It's the injustice of the whole thing that sickens me. Why don't you go home, Fyodor?

KULYGIN *(Kisses her)* You're tired. Rest for half an hour. I'll go downstairs and wait for you. All right? Oh, I'm so happy, happy, happy.

He leaves.

IRINA What did he call Andrey?—'poor old Andrey'. That's accurate enough. Living with that woman has put years on him. I've never known anyone—disintegrate as quickly. Professor Andrey Prozorov! Remember that ambition? And only yesterday he was boasting to me that they've made him permanent on the county council staff, thanks, no doubt, to Mr. Protopopov, the chairman. Why is he so thick? He's the talk of the town. Everybody's laughing at him. Doesn't he see what's happening? And tonight when every other man was out fighting the fire, where's Andrey? Sitting in his room, fiddling! Even to look at him now, just to see what he's become, it's pathetic—it's terrifying. *(Cries)* I don't think I can stand any more. I really don't think I can stand much more. *(OLGA enters.)* I don't think I can carry on much longer, Olga. I've had as much as I can take. I'm beginning to disintegrate too.

OLGA *(Alarmed)* What's wrong, Irina? What's the matter, my darling?

IRINA *(Sobbing)* What's become of everything? Where has it all gone to? Oh my God, I've forgotten everything. Everything's chaotic in my head. What's the Italian word for window—or ceiling? I don't know. It's gone. Every day I forget something more . . . My life, too—haemorrhaging away on me—never to be recovered. And we'll never go to Moscow— never, never, never—I know that now.

OLGA *holds her in her arms and rocks her as she did* ANFISA.

OLGA Shhhhhh, my darling, shush-shush-shush.
IRINA I'm so unhappy, Olga. My God I'm so unhappy. I'm sick working in the county council office. I can't go on working there. I won't go on working there. It's far, far worse than the post-office. I dread and detest every second I spend in it. I'm twenty-three, Olga. I'll soon be twenty-four. And it has all been work, work, work. I've become desiccated in mind and in body. Look at me—I've got thin and ugly and old. I'll soon be twenty-four and what have I to show for it? Nothing, nothing, nothing. And time is slipping away. And every day that races past I feel—I *know* I'm losing touch with everything that has even the smell of hope about it—no, no, even worse than losing touch—sinking, being sucked down into a kind of abyss. I am despairing, Olga. Do you understand what I'm saying? I am desperate. I see no reason to go on living. I see no reason why I shouldn't end it now.
OLGA Don't cry, my darling. Please don't cry. I get so upset when I see you crying.
IRINA I'm not crying. Look—I've stopped. There. No more crying. No more scenes.
OLGA Darling, may I say something to you? May I? The advice of an older sister, the advice of a friend. *(Pause)* You should marry the baron. *(*IRINA *begins crying again quietly.)* Shhhhh. Listen to me. You admire him and you respect him. All right, he may not be the most handsome man in the world, but he is a kind man and he is a decent-minded man, and what you must understand, my darling, what

81

you must learn to accept is that one doesn't marry for love; one marries out of duty. At least that's what I think. I would marry a man I didn't love. I would marry any man who would ask me as long as he was a kind man, a decent man. I would even marry an old man.

IRINA   D'you know what I used to imagine? That when we'd go home to Moscow I'd meet 'the great love of my life'. There he'd be, the man I'd waited for, dreamed of, genuinely loved in anticipation. Wasn't I the fool, the stupid, stupid fool?

OLGA   *(Embracing her)* I know, my darling, I know, I know, I do know. Yes. And I actually cried myself the first time I saw the baron in civilian clothes just after he resigned his commission. He looked so ... ordinary. He asked me why I was crying. And what could I say? But yes, Irina, yes, if he did marry you, if that was the will of God, yes, I'd be happy for you. I would. Because that's really as much as you can hope for now.

NATASHA *enters left, a lit candle in her hand. Without looking left or right she crosses the stage at a brisk pace and exits right.*

MASHA   *(Sitting up)* Would you look at that! Lady Macbeth walks again!

OLGA   *(Laughs)* Masha, you're awful.

MASHA   I wouldn't be surprised if she started the fire.

OLGA   Honest to God, you're the silliest of the three of us.

Pause. MASHA *rises.*

MASHA   There's something I've got to tell you both. General confession time! I want to tell you two and only you two and then I'll never breathe a word of it again to anyone. A secret I want both of you to share. *(Pause. Softly)* I'm in love with Vershinin.

OLGA   You're ——!

MASHA   *(Slightly louder)* I'm in love with Vershinin.

OLGA   Masha, stop that!

MASHA   *(Proclamation)* I am in love with Lieutenant Colonel Alexander Vershinin!

OLGA *dashes behind a screen.*

OLGA Can't hear a word you're saying. Not a single word.

MASHA What am I supposed to do about it? At first I thought he was strange. Then I felt sorry for him. Then I began to love him, love him, love him—love everything about him—the way he walks, the way he talks, his unhappy life, his two little girls ——

OLGA I'm not listening. Talk all the rubbish you want— I'm not listening.

MASHA You're the silly one, Olga. I am in love with Vershinin. There's nothing more to say. Fate, destiny—call it whatever you like. There it is. And he loves me. It's . . . terrifying in a way, isn't it? *(She catches Irina's hands.)* The question is: how are you and I going to live the rest of our lives? What's going to become of us? Like a situation in a novel, isn't it? Except that in a novel it always seems jaded and obvious. But when you fall in love yourself, you're in a situation that you *know* is unique. There are no precedents. There are no guide-lines. You are the first-ever explorer . . . That's all. The general confession. Now I'll keep quiet. Like that madman in Gogol's short story: silence . . . silence . . . shhhhhh.

Enter ANDREY *followed by* FERAPONT.

ANDREY *(Angrily)* What is it? What is it? I don't hear a word you're saying—not a single word!

FERAPONT *(Standing at the door)* I've asked you a dozen times already, Mister Andrey, if you'd ——

ANDREY And don't call me Mister Andrey. Call me Your Honour.

FERAPONT It's the firemen, Mister—Sir—Your Honour—they want to know can they bring their hoses through your garden to the river. They've been lugging them things round the long way all night and you know yourself it takes them twice as ——

ANDREY All right! All right! All right!

FERAPONT Wha's that, Mister—Your Hon- ——?

ANDREY *(Shouts)* All right! Tell them—all right!

83

FERAPONT *leaves.*

ANDREY   Them and their damned hoses! *(To* IRINA*)* Where's Olga?

OLGA *comes from behind the screen.*

ANDREY   I'm looking for the duplicate key of the sideboard. I've lost mine. You know the one I mean. It's about this size and has a brass ——

OLGA *silently holds out a key to him.* IRINA *goes behind a screen. An awkward silence.*

ANDREY   Terrible fire, wasn't it? . . . It's dying down now . . . Poor old Ferapont—did you hear me?—I lost the head with him, told him to address me as Your Honour, for God's sake . . . Why don't you speak, Olga? *(Pause)* Isn't it about time you stopped this silly bloody sulking? If I even knew what you were sulking about! *(Pause)* All right. All right. The three of you are here now—fine—fine—let's clear the air for once and for all. Right. Fine. Now: what have you all got against me?

OLGA   *(Wearily)* Not now, Andrey. Tomorrow maybe. We've all had a bad night.

ANDREY   *(His voice rising)* No need to shout at me. I'm asking a calm, reasonable question—what have you all got against me? I would like a calm, reasonable answer.

VERSHININ   *(Off)* Ta-ra-ra-ra.

MASHA *gets instantly to her feet and responds delightedly.*

MASHA   Ta-ra. Ta-ra. Good night, Olga. Take care of yourself. *(Runs behind the screen and kisses* IRINA.) Sleep well, my darling. *(To* ANDREY *as she rushes past him)* Not tonight, Andrey—they're exhausted. Leave it till tomorrow.

She runs off.

OLGA   Please, Andrey. Leave it till tomorrow. It's time we were all in bed.

She goes behind a screen. Now only ANDREY *is visible.*

ANDREY   I just want to say one thing; then I'll go. Just one thing. Right. Fine. First of all you've got something against my wife, Natasha. I've been aware of this ever since the day we got married. Natasha is a fine, honest, straight-forward, high-principled woman. That is my opinion of her. I love my wife and I respect my wife. Is that clearly understood? I respect my wife and I expect others to respect her too. As I have said, she is a decent woman and a high-principled woman. And your objections to her —whatever those objections are—have no basis whatever in — in — in — in reality. *(He pauses and mops his face with his handkerchief.)* Right. Secondly, you're disappointed in me and annoyed with me because I'm not a professor engaged in academic pursuits. But I happen to work for the county council. I am engaged in public service. And I consider that profession every bit as noble and as honourable as a life in the academy. In point of fact I derive more pride and self-fulfilment from my work in the public interest than I could have had I— have I—had I not been in public service. *(Again he pauses and mops his face with his handkerchief.)* Fine. Right. Thirdly I have something else to say. I know that I mortgaged this house without your permission. I shouldn't have done that. That was wrong of me. I admit that. I apologise. I had to do it because of my debts—I owe thirty-five thousand roubles. I've stopped gambling. I gave it up long ago. And the only excuse I have to offer is that you girls get the annuity father left you whereas I have no income—I mean to say no inherited income.

KULYGIN   *(Off)* Masha? Masha? *(His head around the door.)* Where's Masha? Isn't she here? I left her sleeping there. Good heavens, that's strange! *(He exits.)*

Pause.

ANDREY *(Softly, wearily)* They won't listen to me. I'm telling you: Natasha is a good wife and a good mother; she is a fine woman, a decent woman, a high-principled . . .

He begins to cry. He tries to stop but cannot. He sinks down on to the edge of the couch, slides off it and is now on his knees, facing upstage, sobbing helplessly.

ANDREY When we got married I thought we would be happy . . . all of us . . . together . . . happy . . . Oh my God . . . My dear sisters, my darling sisters, everything I've said is lies . . . everything . . . Don't believe a word of it . . . not a single word . . .

Pause. Then he gets quickly to his feet and stumbles off.

KULYGIN *(Head around the door and now very agitated)* Where *is* Masha? She's not downstairs. She's not here. Where *is* she? Extraordinary—that's what it is!

He exits. Fire alarm off. The stage is empty. Silence. Then IRINA *and* OLGA *talk behind their screens.*

IRINA Olga.
OLGA Yes?
IRINA Who's that knocking on the floor?
OLGA The doctor. He's drunk.
IRINA God. What a night. *(Pause)* Olga.
OLGA What?

IRINA *now appears from behind her screen. She is in her nightdress.*

IRINA Did you hear the news? They're moving our brigade. They're being sent to some place far away.
OLGA That's only a rumour.
IRINA We'll be all on our own then, Olga.
OLGA So.

Pause.

IRINA I do respect the baron, Olga, I do, honestly. I have a very high opinion of him. I think he is a very . . . worthy man. And I *will* marry him, Olga, I will, I will, if we can go to Moscow then. I'm asking you, Olga—I'm begging you—please. Let us go to Moscow. There's nowhere in the world like Moscow. Let us go, Olga. Please, let us go.

BRING DOWN LIGHTS SLOWLY
END OF ACT THREE

ACT FOUR

Almost two years have passed. Autumn. Noon. Diluted sunshine—the first snow of winter is imminent.

The old garden of the Prozorov house. Stage left a garden swing. Stage right the verandah of the house. On the verandah a table with glasses and empty champagne bottles. In the distance a long avenue of fir trees beyond which one can see the river. Beyond the river is a wood.

CHEBUTYKIN *sits at the table, drinks champagne, and reads his paper. He is in a benevolent mood which lasts throughout the entire Act. He is waiting to be summoned for the duel. His army cap and stick on the table beside him.*

IRINA, KULYGIN *(wearing a decoration round his neck and with his moustache shaved off) and* TUSENBACH *emerge from the house.* FEDOTIK *and* RODDEY *are with them. They all stand on the steps of the verandah to say goodbye.* FEDOTIK *and* RODDEY *are in field uniform.*

BARON	*(Embracing FEDOTIK)* We had a lot of fun together, Fedotik. I m going to miss you. *(He now embraces* RODDEY.*)* You, too, Roddey. Goodbye, friends. Goodbye, old comrades.
IRINA	It's not goodbye. It's au revoir.
FEDOTIK	It's goodbye and well you know it.
RODDEY	*(About to cry)* Please, my petals . . . please . . .
FEDOTIK	We'll never see each other again.
KULYGIN	You don't know that. *(Wiping his eyes; to* RODDEY*)* Now you have me crying too.
IRINA	Yes, we all *will* meet again. I know we will.
FEDOTIK	*(Lining up camera shot)* Maybe in ten or fifteen years time. And by then we'd be strangers. We wouldn't even recognise one another. Hold it like that!
RODDEY	Oh my goodness me!
FEDOTIK	*(Flash)* Lovely.
RODDEY	'Lovely', he says! How can I be lovely when my eyes are all blotchy!
FEDOTIK	And another, please—just one more—the last one. You all look so distinguished.
RODDEY	Who wants to look distinguished! We just want to look pretty! *(Another camera flash. Embracing* TUSENBACH.*)* We'll never meet again, Baron. Goodbye, my friend, and great good luck—*(He kisses*

IRINA)—to both of you. May you have every happiness together, Irina, and may all your troubles be little ones—if you like that sort of thing. I—I—I ——

He is overcome and rushes upstage.

FEDOTIK Hold on, Roddey! I'm coming!

BARON Irina's right: we *will* meet again. I'm sure we will. And in the meantime you'll write to us both, won't you? That's a promise.

RODDEY *(Going round garden)* Goodbye, trees. *(Shouts)* Goodbye!

ECHO Bye-bye-bye . . .

RODDEY *(Shouts)* Goodbye, echo.

ECHO Echo-echo-echo . . .

KULYGIN *(To* FEDOTIK*)* You'll not be three months in Poland till you find yourself a splendid Polish wife. And every night she'll throw her arms around you and whisper 'Kohany'.

FEDOTIK *(Pretended shock)* Kulygin!

KULYGIN *(Confused)* It means—it simply means 'beloved'—that's all.

FEDOTIK Ah. *(Looks at his watch.)* Less than an hour to go. Solyony's the only man from our battery going on the barge. We're with the men. Three battery divisions move out today; three more tomorrow. Then the town will return to peace and quiet again.

TUSENBACH Boredom's more like it. Sheer damned bordeom.

RODDEY *(Upstage)* Where's Masha?

KULYGIN In the garden somewhere.

FEDOTIK We must say goodbye to her.

RODDEY 'Bye, everyone.

He looks back at them. Then on impulse he returns to them, embracing TUSENBACH *and* KULYGIN *and kissing Irina's hand—all exactly as before.*

RODDEY My darlings, my petals, can you believe it's been almost five years?—five wonderful, sensational, fantastic years—that's what it has all been—just incredible. I'll remember every detail for—for—for as long as ——

89

FEDOTIK *(To* KULYGIN; *a pen)* A little souvenir for you, Kulygin, to ——

RODDEY *(Irritably, in tears)* Toys! Toys! When are you going to grow up!

And again he rushes upstage.

FEDOTIK It's a miniature pen and note-book. Something to remember me by.

KULYGIN I'm really most ——

FEDOTIK *(Now embarrassed)* This is the quickest way back, isn't it?

He joins RODDEY. *They both begin to leave together.*

RODDEY *(Shouts)* 'Bye!

ECHO Bye-bye-bye . . .

KULYGIN *(Shouts)* Goodbye!

As they exit they meet MASHA. *All three leave together. Brief pause.*

IRINA That's the end of that.

She sits on the verandah steps.

CHEBUTYKIN They forgot to say goodbye to me.

IRINA Did you say goodbye to them?

CHEBUTYKIN Good point. Sympathetic amnesia. Is that the word —amnesia? Sounds strange. 'Amnesia'. Is that a word at all? Anyhow I'll be seeing them before long. I'm off tomorrow. One more day left here. But when I get my pension in twelve months time I'll come back and spend the remainder of my days here with you. Straight back to the sun like a migrating bird. And I'll be so changed, you won't know me. I'll be a quiet, benign, *(lifting his glass)* and totally abstemious old gentleman.

IRINA We certainly won't know you.

CHEBUTYKIN Well, the aspiration at least is noble, isn't it? *(Sings softly)* 'There was I, waiting at the church, waiting at the church, waiting at the ——'

KULYGIN	You're incorrigible, doctor.
CHEBUTYKIN	Am I? Maybe you should take me in hand. Would that have any effect?
IRINA	*(To* CHEBUTYKIN*)* Fyodor's shaved off his moustache. *(To* KULYGIN*)* I like you the way you were.
KULYGIN	Did you? What's wrong with it now?
IRINA	I just think you're . . . I much preferred you the way you were.
KULYGIN	Really? Well, this is the new style. Moustaches are out. Our headmaster got rid of his, and the day I was appointed assistant-head, off went mine. Oddly enough nobody seems to like it. Not that that matters. I'm perfectly happy. With a moustache—without a moustache—I'm perfectly . . .

He fades out, stands irresolutely for a second, and sits. ANDREY *enters, his nose deep in a book, pushing a pram. He crosses the back of the stage and exits. Pause. Then* IRINA *goes to the doctor.*

IRINA	Dear, darling, dopey doctor ——
CHEBUTYKIN	You haven't called me that in ages.
IRINA	I'm worried sick.
CHEBUTYKIN	My own little sweetheart, what is it?
IRINA	You were in town last night, weren't you?
CHEBUTYKIN	I was.
IRINA	What happened?
CHEBUTYKIN	What do you mean?
IRINA	Outside the theatre—there was a row of some sort.
CHEBUTYKIN	Was there?
IRINA	You know there was. Between the baron and Solyony.
CHEBUTYKIN	Oh, that.
IRINA	What happened?
CHEBUTYKIN	That was nothing. *(Opens his paper.)* Nothing. Hot air. Big words. Nothing. Nothing.
KULYGIN	The story I heard was that just as the baron came out of the theatre he met Solyony by accident and for no apparent reason Solyony squared up to him and ——
TUSENBACH	Stop it, will you! Stop it! Stop it! *(Now controlled).* It's nobody's business but mine and ——

He rushes into the house.

KULYGIN Solyony began picking on him. The baron got
angry, insulted Solyony. And the two of them ——

CHEBUTYKIN Were you there?

KULYGIN No.

CHEBUTYKIN All you know is what you've picked up from gossip
—isn't that right?

KULYGIN I suppose so.

CHEBUTYKIN Anyhow, the whole thing—it's ridiculous, just
ridiculous. Two supposedly adult people behaving
like—like—like—Ridiculous!

KULYGIN Interesting Latin word that—'ridiculus'. From the
verb rideo-ridere-risi-risum, meaning to laugh.
Hence ridicule, ridiculous, risible etc. etc. Which
reminds me of a very comical anecdote—this is
really 'risible', you'll love this, Irina—a story of a
teacher who wrote on the bottom of a student's
Latin composition—"Ridiculous"—'ous', the Eng-
lish ending. But the poor student took it to be the
Latin 'us' and declined it! Oh my goodness, I love
that story! *(Pause)* Actually the gossip is—if you'll
pardon me, doctor—the gossip is that Solyony's in
love with Irina! Yes! And *that's* why he detests the
baron. That's the rumour. And that's perfectly
understandable—I mean that he loves Irina, not
that he detests the baron! Because Irina is a wonder-
ful human being. Oh, yes, you are. In many respects
very like my Masha. The same pensive nature. But
you're not as—as—as introspective as Masha.
You're more outgoing. Though Masha on occasion
and in a certain humour, my Masha can indeed be
very, very outgoing herself. Oh, I do love Masha.

From off stage the sound of FEDOTIK *calling*
'Goodbye' *and the echoing answers of* 'Bye-bye-
bye . . .' *They listen until the last sound dies away.*

IRINA *(Shivering)* Something eerie about that sound.
Everything seems to frighten me today. *(Rapidly
and with sudden desperate resolution)* Well, at least
everything's organised. My stuff's all packed and
goes off on the evening train; and tomorrow

morning immediately after the wedding the baron and I go straight to the brick-works—just like your migrating bird, except of course that we're heading north, away from the sun. And the morning after that I begin my first teaching job. One-two-three—just like that—wife, teacher, and a whole new life all in the space of three hectic days. But Olga assures me everything's in God's hands. And Olga must be right, mustn't she? . . . The day I got my teaching diploma I was so happy I—I cried . . .

CHEBUTYKIN is deeply moved. He goes to her and puts his arms around her.

CHEBUTYKIN My own little sweetheart . . . my tiny white bird . . . Of course you're going to fly away to the sun, up and away with the great blue sky above you and other beautiful white birds all around you. Of course you will. Fly away, my sweetheart. For God's sake soar away up there while you're still young. Do it now, now, fly now, or you'll never do it. What's here is only fit for old moulting things that can't keep up with the flock any more. *(Into her ear)* He's not telling the truth. He didn't shave off that moustache. He's moulting too.

KULYGIN The Order of Saint Stanislaus, second class. You've seen my decoration, doctor, haven't you?

CHEBUTYKIN Once or twice.

The sound of somebody playing The Maiden's Prayer *on the piano off.*

KULYGIN 'For dutiful service to the cause of education'. I'm wearing it today to celebrate the . . . military withdrawal and our return to the way things used to be. I'm all for routine. There's a lot to be said for routine. 'For dutiful service' . . . All things considered I suppose I'm a very fortunate man. I enjoy my work, exhausting though it may be. And I have my Masha, my loyal and faithful Masha—despite suggestions to the contrary. Yes, I suppose people would consider me a very fortunate man. I'm sure they would. I mean to say, why wouldn't they? Yes, indeed, why wouldn't they? . . .

As before he tails off into a private misery. Pause.

IRINA This time tomorrow night I won't be listening to *The Maiden's Prayer*.

CHEBUTYKIN Lucky girl. Or seeing Mister Protopopov ensconsed in the drawingroom with Natasha.

IRINA Shhh. He's in there now.

CHEBUTYKIN Isn't he always?

KULYGIN Where's Olga? Has the new headmistress not arrived yet?

IRINA She'll be here soon. Lucky Olga, living in that school-house. I envy her living there. It has been very lonely here without her. And I envy her her full, busy life. I hate this house without her. I've been relegated to the back-bedroom—did you know that? Hate it and bored by it. But I am becoming . . . 'reconciled'—isn't that the word, doctor?

ANDREY *enters with his book and pram.*

CHEBUTYKIN No, no, no. Fly, white bird. Fly.

IRINA 'Realistic'—maybe that's more accurate. Because if I can't go to Moscow, I must accept that Moscow's out. That is God's will and I really believe that. *(Pause)* So, when the baron asked me to marry him, I thought it over and I said yes, yes I would marry him. Because he is a kind man, a genuinely good man, a decent-minded man. And that's the kind of husband every girl ought to marry. So I said yes, yes. And the moment I made that decision, the moment I said yes to him, a lot of the confusion seemed to lift and I felt a great sense of relief and the old passion for work, work, work suddenly possessed me again. Life had acquired a fresh pattern; a new shape was emerging. I really think I was almost happy again. And then this morning, when I heard about that incident outside the theatre last night, the confusion descended again and I have a sense that something eerie is going to happen, something sinister.

94

CHEBUTYKIN	Rubbish. For God's sake ——
NATASHA	*(At the window)* The headmistress is here!
KULYGIN	Ah! Olga's arrived. Let's go outside. She'll have all the news about her staff.

He leads IRINA *into the house. The doctor pours himself a drink, checks the time, and opens his paper, all the time singing* 'There was I, waiting at the church, waiting at the church, waiting at the church . . .' MASHA *enters.*

MASHA	You look very comfortable sitting there.
CHEBUTYKIN	And why not? Sit down here. What's happening?
MASHA	What in God's name could be happening? Not a single thing's happening. *(Pause)* Were you in love with my mother? *(Pause)* Doctor.
CHEBUTYKIN	*(Simply)* Desperately.
MASHA	Was she in love with you?
CHEBUTYKIN	I don't remember—where's Vershinin?
MASHA	He's on his way. *(Pause)* When you've had to snatch at whatever happiness you can in furtive little grabs and then lose it all, as I've lost it all, you become hard and bitter. *(Calmly and softly)* I am seething inside, doctor.

ANDREY, *who has been standing and reading, moves slowly across the back of the stage.*

MASHA	Look at him—once the repository of all our aspirations. The eminently eligible Andrey Prozorov— academician, musician, gentleman about town. There's a defeat for you, doctor; there's an unconditional surrender.

A sudden loud sound of dishes falling and smashing off and of maids shouting at one another.

ANDREY	Is this racket never going to stop for God's sake! When are we going to get some peace in this house!
MASHA	There go all our hopes.
CHEBUTYKIN	I wonder what's keeping them?
MASHA	What's keeping who?
CHEBUTYKIN	*(Looking at his watch)* Nice old-fashioned watch,

isn't it? Listen. *(He presses a button on it. The watch chimes.)*

MASHA You're up to something. What is it?

ANDREY *moves down beside them.*

CHEBUTYKIN The First, Second and Fifth batteries are pulling out at one o'clock sharp. I leave tomorrow.

ANDREY For good?

CHEBUTYKIN Most likely. I don't know. Maybe I'll come back in a year's time. God alone knows. Does it matter?

A harp and a violin in the far distance play 'Won't You Buy My Pretty Flowers?'

ANDREY The town'll seem deserted now. Now we'll really go to seed. *(He puts down his book and removes his glasses.)* By the way what happened outside the theatre last night?

CHEBUTYKIN Nothing. Sheer stupidity. Solyony said something that angered the baron. The baron flared up and insulted Solyony. One word led to another and the outcome was that Solyony had to challenge him to a duel. *(Looks at watch.)* It's about to begin; 12.30 in the forest, just across the river there. Bang-bang. *(Laughs)* Did you know that Solyony imagines he's like Lermontov, the writer? I'm serious. He even writes poetry! Joking apart though, this is his third duel.

MASHA They ought to be stopped.

CHEBUTYKIN D'you think so?

MASHA He might wound the baron. He might even kill him.

CHEBUTYKIN That's true, he might. And the baron's not a bad sort. But one baron more or less in the world— does that matter? Let them tear away. Who cares?

Shouts from the distance: 'Hello, there! Hello! Hello!'

CHEBUTYKIN *(Quietly)* Oh, shut up! That's Skvorstsov calling the boat. He's one of Solyony's seconds.

ANDREY *steels himself to make a pronouncement.*

96

ANDREY   I'm no expert in ethics. But it is absolutely crystal
         clear to me that—that—that ——

CHEBUTYKIN   That what?

> MASHA *drifts into a reverie and hums her Masha-
> Vershinin theme.* ANDREY *is faltering, partly be-
> cause he is distracted by Masha's humming.*

ANDREY   Well, it would seem to be obvious—fairly obvious—
         at least it would appear to me to be reasonable to
         suggest that—that ——

CHEBUTYKIN   That what?

ANDREY   That to fight a duel, even to attend a duel, even as
         a doctor, maybe especially as a doctor, is—is—is
         immoral. That's what.

CHEBUTYKIN   Immoral?

ANDREY   Immoral.

CHEBUTYKIN   Do you think so?

ANDREY   Yes. That's what I think. Yes. That's how it seems
         to me.

CHEBUTYKIN   Ah! That's how it 'seems' to you. But we don't exist.

ANDREY   We ——?

CHEBUTYKIN   We're not real at all. Nothing in the world is real.
         It only seems to us that we exist. And this brings us
         right into the heart of the matter: the distinction
         between essence and existence. But how are we com-
         petent to make that distinction until we first deter-
         mine whether we exist or don't exist?

ANDREY   I—I ——

CHEBUTYKIN   And even if we were to determine that, finally,
         finally does it all matter one—little—whit?

MASHA   Talk—talk—talk. Nothing but talk the whole damn
        day long. *(She moves towards the house.)* As if this
        bloody awful climate with snow about to fall any
        minute weren't enough to endure, we have to listen
        to all this blathering!

> She is about to go into the house when she is
> arrested by Natasha's stilted laughter and her line

NATASHA   Where's your manners, Bobik! Say, 'Goodday,
          Mister Protopopov'.

MASHA   Christ! Is there nowhere to go! *(She moves up the*

97

garden, stops, calls back.) Let me know when Vershinin comes, will you? *(She looks up at the sky.)* Look. The swans are escaping south already. Lucky, happy, happy, lucky swans.

She goes off.

ANDREY *moves beside* CHEBUTYKIN *and sits down.*

ANDREY With the officers gone and you gone and Irina getting married I'll be alone here.
CHEBUTYKIN What about your wife?
ANDREY What about my wife. *(He shrugs.)* She's my wife. What else is there to say? She looks after me well. My wife looks after me well. My wife is a fine woman. My wife is an honest, straight-forward, high-principled woman. Oh dear God . . . May I tell you about my wife, doctor? May I talk to you in confidence as a doctor, as a friend? My wife is an animal—a mean, myopic, gross, grubbing animal. There's not a trace of humanity left in her. And yet—and yet—and yet—having said all that, I still love her, doctor. God-damnit, I love her, *love* her for God's sake, love her despite her vulgarity, despite everything that she is, everything she does, despite everything that's despicable in her. So I suppose all I'm really saying to you is that I'm so bewildered I don't know what I think any more. And God alone knows why I still love her, if I still love her . . . It doesn't make much sense, does it? *(Natasha's loud laughter off.)* I suppose what I'm trying to say to you is that I don't think I can stand any more. I—I—I'm desperate, doctor.
CHEBUTYKIN *(Rising)* I'm going away tomorrow, Andrey. The chances are we'll never meet again. So I *will* give you my advice. Put on your hat, take up your walking-stick, and leave.
ANDREY *(Astonished, terrified)* Leave! But ——
CHEBUTYKIN And the further you go, the better.

SOLYONY *enters resolutely, crossing upstage with his second. He sees* CHEBUTYKIN *and comes down to him. The second goes off.* SOLYONY *is both icy and elated.*

SOLYONY	Twelve-thirty, doctor. Time to go.
CHEBUTYKIN	Coming—coming—coming. God, I'm sick of you all. *(To* ANDREY*)* If anybody asks where I am, just say I'll be back soon. *(He goes to* ANDREY, *embraces him very warmly, and releases him.)* Oh dear, oh dear, oh dear.

FERAPONT *enters and waits his chance to address* ANDREY.

SOLYONY	What are you lamenting about, old man? 'Tweedle-de-dum and tweedle-de-dee, Is there a bird as happy as we?'
CHEBUTYKIN	*(Leaving)* Come on.
SOLYONY	Aren't you looking forward to it?
CHEBUTYKIN	I can hardly wait!
SOLYONY	All right—all right—keep calm. I'm not going to do the big job on him. Just wing him—the way I'd bring down a woodcock. *(Sprinking his hands with perfume.)* I've used up a whole bottle already today and they still smell of . . . decay. Is that an omen? 'But he rebellious, seeks the storm / As if in storms lay peace.' Lermontov. D'you know that poem?
CHEBUTYKIN	Of course. How's this it goes? 'There was I waiting at the church, waiting at the church, waiting at the church . . .'

CHEBUTYKIN *and* SOLYONY *leave together.*

SOLYONY	*(Off, shouting)* Hello, Skvorstsov! Hello, there!
VOICE	*(Off, shouting)* Hello! Hello!

FERAPONT *moves down beside* ANDREY.

FERAPONT	Excuse me, Sir. I've some papers here for you to sign, if you ——
ANDREY	Leave me alone, will you? Will you for God's sake leave me alone!

ANDREY *goes off rapidly with the pram.*

FERAPONT	What am I to do with these papers? I mean, like, if

official papers aren't signed, what's to become of them?

He follows ANDREY *off.* IRINA *and* TUSENBACH *enter from the house. The* BARON *is wearing a straw hat. Just as they enter* KULYGIN *crosses the back of the stage, calling softly and anxiously.*

KULYGIN Masha? Ma-sha! Where are you, Masha?

BARON He'll be the only person in the town who'll be glad to see the army leaving.

IRINA Would you blame him? *(Pause)* The town'll die now.

BARON I'll be back in a minute, my darling.

IRINA Where are you going?

BARON Just down to the camp—just to say goodbye to the men.

IRINA You're not telling me the truth, Nikolay. What happened outside the theatre last night?

BARON Half an hour—give me half an hour and I'll be straight back to you. *(He takes her hand and kisses it.)* My beautiful Irina. *(Holds her in his arms.)* Five years since I first fell in love with you—five years!—and I'm still surprised, amazed, staggered by it all. Every day, every hour of every day you become more and more beautiful, more and more exquisite. And tomorrow I'll take you away from here and we'll marry and we'll work and we'll be rich and everything I ever dreamed of will be realised. And you'll be happy too, because I'll ——

IRINA Nikolay, I ——

He puts his hand across her mouth.

BARON I know—shhhh—I know—I know—only just don't say it—please. But you do *like* me all right, don't you? I mean you don't dislike me—I know you don't. And in time, my darling, in time, in time what you do like about me may grow and blossom and you'll get to like me more and more. And in time, in time—give it time—you may even begin to—to love me just a little bit . . . to coin a phrase . . .

100

IRINA I *do* like you, Nikolay. You know I like you very much. And I will marry you and honour you and obey you; and that won't be difficult because I am very fond of you. But I don't love you, Nikolay. That's something I can't summon. *(She begins to cry)* I've never been in love. I've dreamed about it all my life. But it has never happened to me. Sometimes I think that all that's needed is the magic key, the code, the password—and suddenly all that pentup, waiting love will spill out . . . I know something's wrong. Tell me what it is.

BARON I didn't sleep last night. Thinking about that elusive key. Irina, say something encouraging to me— please—anything.

IRINA What can I say?

BARON A phrase—a word—a look ——

IRINA I can't—I can't—you know I can't ——

Suddenly Solyony's shout, now further away. The BARON *responds.*

SOLYONY Hello, there!

VOICE Hello! Hello!

Pause.

BARON *(Almost to himself)* Strange thing is that in the end it's never the great passions, the great ambitions that determine the course our lives take, but some trivial, piddling little thing that we dismiss and refuse to take seriously; until it's too late. And then we recognise that the piddling little thing has manipulated us into a situation that is irrevocable and . . . final.

IRINA *(Anxiously)* It's to do with Solyony! That's what happened outside the theatre—you and Solyony are ——

BARON *(Delighted)* There! Concern! You're concerned for me! You can't hide it! And suddenly I feel elated— no, exalted! I love you! I love life! I love everybody and everything! Look at those fir-trees, those maples, those birches—I've never seen them before! Aren't they beautiful? And look, Irina—they're

looking back at me—they're alert—they're watch-
ful—they're waiting for something to happen. Aren't
they beautiful? Aren't they wise? With beautiful,
wise trees like that around you, life should be
beautiful too!

SOLYONY *(Far off)* Hello!
VOICE *(Far off)* Hello! Hello!

Again the Baron's mood changes.

BARON I have to go now. Look—there's a tree that's dead.
But it's still swaying in the breeze with the others.
I have that sense about myself too: that even if I
die, somehow or other I'll still be part of life.
Goodbye, my darling.

IRINA Nikolay, I ——

BARON Shhhhhh. *(He kisses her hand.)* The postcards you
sent me each summer—there are three of them—
they're in the top drawer of my desk.

IRINA I'm going with you.

BARON *(Quietly, firmly)* No, no. You're staying here. *(He
moves briskly away and stops before exiting.)* Irina.

IRINA Yes? *(Pause. He stares strangely at her.)* What is it,
Nikolay?

BARON I—I—I didn't get a cup of coffee this morning.
Would you ask them to get some for me?

*He leaves. She stares after him, then goes to the
swing and sits there encased in her own thoughts.*
ANDREY *with his book and pram enters, followed
by* FERAPONT.

FERAPONT Mister Andrey, Sir, these papers aren't mine, you
know; they're official papers. I didn't invent them.

ANDREY *now addresses* FERAPONT *as he did in
Act Two, speaking very softly, almost in quiet
soliloquy.*

ANDREY D'you know what I find difficult to believe,
Ferapont? I can hardly convince myself now that
there *was* a time in my life when I was young and
happy and eager, when I had noble dreams and

noble ambitions, when the future was almost breathless with hope. That really puzzles me. Because there was such a time, wasn't there? Yes, there must have been. But if there was, why can't I remember it? How could it just vanish so completely? And why is it, Ferapont, that at a certain point in our lives—there we are, young, bright, eager, just about to inherit the earth—why is it that instead of fulfilling those hopes and ambitions, instead of taking possession of that waiting world, we suddenly become weary and dull and apathetic? Why is that? I wonder why that is. Look at this town. One hundred thousand people—all indistinguishable. In the two hundred years this town has been in existence, it hasn't produced one person of any distinction—not one saint, not one scholar, not one artist. Just one hundred thousand identical, drab people, eating, sleeping, working, eating, sleeping, dying. Isn't it puzzling? And in order to invest their drab lives with some little excitement, they gossip and drink and gamble and take each other to court for broken fences and for slander actions—because if they didn't, they'd die of overwhelming boredom. Yes, die of it. That's why wives deceive their husbands—not for pleasure but just to reassure themselves they are still alive. And that's why husbands pretend they hear nothing and see nothing. Their very pretence is an activity, an assertion—no, a faint whisper—that they're alive too. Isn't it ridiculous? And into this charade children are born with their own hopes and their own dreams and then in time succumb like the rest of us to this living death, become spectres like the rest of us. It's all absurd. Can I help you?

FERAPONT These papers still have to be signed.

ANDREY *(Without impatience)* You're a pest, Ferapont.

FERAPONT *hands over the papers.*

FERAPONT The porter in the tax office told me a terrific story this morning.

ANDREY *(Leafing through the papers)* Yes.

103

FERAPONT He told me that in Petersburg last winter they had two hundred degrees of frost!

ANDREY But there is the tiniest glimmer of hope still, Ferapont. We have got to keep believing that all this squalor, all this degradation—this endless round of vodka and cabbage-and-bacon and gossip and pretence—it will end soon and we must keep believing in a future for our children that is open and honest and free. Because the very fact of clinging on to that belief is in itself the beginning of a release, a liberation. Maybe the only liberation available to us . . . *(With failing conviction)* Anyhow, that's what I believe. That's what I believe passionately. I'm firmly, absolutely firmly convinced of that, Ferapont—absolutely . . .

FERAPONT Two hundred people froze to death that winter. And d'you know what the porter said? Hee-hee-hee. He said everyone was scared 'stiff'!

ANDREY I know it's no excuse at all, Ferapont, but I haven't got a hat or a walking-stick . . .

He begins to cry, at first gently, and then sobbing uncontrollably. He tries to hide from FERAPONT *by covering his face with his hands.* FERAPONT *watches him blankly.*

ANDREY My dear sisters . . . my wonderful sisters . . . Masha, my darling sister . . .

Pause. Then Natasha's head appears at the window.

NATASHA Who's making that racket out there? Is it you, Andrey? Sweet mother of God, how can wee Sophie sleep with a racket like that? *(Controlled again)* Il ne faut pas faire du bruit, la Sophie est dormée déjà. Vous êtes un ours. *(Furious again)* If you can't keep your big mouth shut, let someone else mind the wane. You there, Ferapont, take that pram away from Mister Prozorov!

FERAPONT Yes, Ma'am. Certainly, Ma'am.

She withdraws. FERAPONT *takes the pram.*

ANDREY I didn't think I was making any . . .

He tails off. Picks up the papers.

NATASHA *(Off)* Bobik! Bobik! Don't you dare spit into Mr. Protopopov's good hat! Don't you dare, you naughty little rascal!

ANDREY I'll go through these tonight and sign the ones that need signing.

FERAPONT Wha's that, Sir?

ANDREY *(Quietly)* I'll have them ready for you tomorrow . . . *(as he leaves)* . . . or the day after . . .

FERAPONT *wheels the pram off.*

NATASHA *(Off)* Now, Bobik, who's this—eh? Bobik, stop that! That's dirty, dirty, dirty! Now, darling, who's this? You know who it is. It's Auntie Olga. Say 'Good afternoon, Auntie Olga'.

While NATASHA *is talking two itinerant musicians enter, an old man and his daughter. He is the violinist and she the harpist. They look around.* VERSHININ, OLGA *and* ANFISA *enter from the house.*

OLGA Our garden's become like a public road—everybody seems to walk through it. Nanny, give those musicians something.

IRINA *leaves her swing and joins the others.* ANFISA, *now much more assured and confident than in Act Three, gives money to the musicians.*

ANFISA There you are. Thank you. Off you go. *(The musicians leave.)* God help them, the creatures; sure if they had a full stomach, they wouldn't be jouking about the countryside like that. *(Now seeing* IRINA *for the first time)* Irina! My wee pet! How are you?

They kiss and embrace.

IRINA You're looking great, Nanny.

ANFISA And why wouldn't I? Sure aren't we as happy as a

105

pair of pups together! And amn't I living the life of a queen? You'll have to come and see it for yourself: the flat's as big as a palace and it's right beside the school and from the kitchen window I can see Olga in her classroom and it's as bright and as sunny and as warm and as dry—*(To* OLGA*)* isn't it? And you'll never guess, love: I've a lovely big room of my own—*(To* OLGA*)* haven't I? The warmest and brightest room in the flat! Looking out over the playground. All for nothing—all paid for by the Department of Education—free! Didn't we fall on our feet? Thanks be to God, thanks be to almighty God, but He's made me a very contented aul' woman in my old age, far more contented than I've a right to be or expect. D'you know, darling, sometimes I wake up in the middle of the night and I think to myself, I think to myself: Thanks be to God and His holy mother, I'm the happiest aul' woman in the world.

IRINA I'm delighted for you, Nanny. I really am delighted.
VERSHININ We're about to leave, Olga. I've got to run. *(Shakes her hand.)* I hope you get even some of the happiness *you* deserve . . . Have you any idea where Masha is?
IRINA She's about somewhere. I'll get her.
VERSHININ Thanks. I'm late already.
ANFISA Sure you couldn't find your right hand. I'll get her. Masha? Masha!

ANFISA *goes off.* IRINA *smiles at the others and follows.*

VERSHININ *(Looking at his watch)* We've just been at the town-hall . . . farewell lunch of sorts . . . champagne, the usual . . . the mayor made a long speech . . . toasts . . . I'm not too sure what happened. My mind was here all the time. I never seem to be away from here.

He looks round anxiously for MASHA.

OLGA Will we ever see each other again?
VERSHININ Most unlikely, isn't it? *(Pause)* My wife and my two little girls are staying on for a while, until I can

send for them. Maybe if they need anything, or if anything were to happen, would it be too much trouble to ——

OLGA Of course, of course. Don't worry about that. I'll take care of them.

VERSHININ Thank you.

OLGA It'll be strange not to see military uniforms on the streets from tomorrow on. All we'll have is our memories of you. We'll have to begin putting a new life together . . . Nothing ever turns out the way we want it to, does it? I never wanted to be a headmistress and now I'm a headmistress. I did want to go home to Moscow and now I never will go home to Moscow.

She is about to cry and to hide her embarrassment she imitates Vershinin's gesture of spreading her hands.

OLGA Well . . .

He mimes the gesture back.

VERSHININ I know. Anyway thank you for everything. And sorry for boring you with my endless talk. I talk too much, far too much, I know I do. And thank you too, Olga, for being so . . . tolerant. I know you've always disapproved strongly of—of—of the relationship between Masha and ——

OLGA *(Drying her eyes, very briskly)* What *is* keeping her?

An awkward silence.

VERSHININ I'm sure I must have some final 'philosophical' gem to impart in the last minute. Surely to God I'm not tongue-tied! *(Laughs uneasily.)* Let's see. 'Life is not a bed of roses. Indeed it may appear to many to be totally bleak and hopeless. But there is evidence, however slender, that it is improving. And perhaps the time is not too far away when it may be described as almost hopeful.' What about that? *(Looks at his watch.)* I really can't stay much longer. All the same there *has* been a great improve-

107

ment in the 'human condition' or whatever you want to call it. What we forget is that there was a time when man's entire existence was taken up with the search for food and shelter, with cultivating a patch of land and defending it against intruders, with feeding and clothing himself and his family. At least we have moved forward from that. And now that those basic concerns have been taken care of, those pressures removed, there is a great void, a great emptiness in man's life, and he's searching for something to fill it. He doesn't know yet what it is he wants. But he's seeking and he will find it. He'll find it soon. But until he does, my solution for his sense of emptiness is a combination of two things: education and work, hard work and education. The solution according to Vershinin . . . *(He laughs, then mocks himself with his gesture.)* Well . . . I warned you there was a final lecture left in me. *(Looks at watch.)* I've really got to go.

OLGA Here she is.

MASHA enters.

VERSHININ I came to say goodbye.

OLGA moves upstage.

MASHA Goodbye.

Pause as they look at each other. Then suddenly they embrace. A long kiss. OLGA looks away.

OLGA Please! Please! For God's sake—please!

MASHA sobs loudly.

VERSHININ Write to me, my darling. And when you think about me —— *(MASHA flings her arms around him. Pause.)* I have got to leave now, Masha. Olga, please. I must go. I'm late already.

OLGA takes MASHA, still sobbing, in her arms.

108

VERSHININ *takes Olga's free hand and kisses it.*
Then he leaves. MASHA *emits a long, loud anguished*
howl.

OLGA Shhhhh, my darling, please . . . please, my darling,
shhh . . .

KULYGIN *enters. Hs is so embarrassed, so totally*
defeated, that even his clichéd and protective speech
patterns fail him. He cries quietly. As he cries

KULYGIN Let her cry . . . doesn't matter . . . let her cry . . .
doesn't matter at all . . . My Masha, my good kind
Masha, you are my wife and I am happy no matter
what . . . Oh Jesus Christ . . . I'm not complaining
—really I'm not—not blaming you at all—not in
the slightest. Isn't that right, Olga? Have I ever
complained, Olga? Ever? What we'll do is—what
we'll have to do is—we'll have to go back to the
way we used to be before—before—And I promise
you, my darling, I promise you I'll never ever make
any reference to—to—ever say a single word
about—about . . .

He breaks down.

MASHA 'A green oak grows by a curving shore
And on that oak a gold chain hangs;
And on that oak a gold chain hangs . . .'
I think I'm going mad, Olga. 'A green oak grows
by a curving shore . . .'
OLGA Shhhh, my love, shhhh—easy, easy—don't talk—
(To KULYGIN*)*—a glass of water.
MASHA No more crying.
KULYGIN No more crying. All over and done with. All
finished.

Distant sound of a gunshot.

MASHA 'A green oak hangs by a golden shore—a hanging
shore—And on that chain a green oak curves—a
green chain curves—a gold oak hangs ——' I've
got it all mixed up. *(Drinks water.)* It's all a mess,

all a confusion. Just give me a minute—I'll be all
right in a minute. No more crying. What's that line
again? 'A green oak hangs by a golden shore'—
what's that supposed to mean? If I can't get those
lines out of my head, Olga, I think I'll go mad.

IRINA *enters.*

OLGA No, you won't. You're better already. You're fine
now.

MASHA No more crying.

OLGA Good. Now, give me your hand. We'll go inside
together.

MASHA *(With sudden anger and lucidity)* I am not going into
that house! *(Sobbing again, softly)* I'm not going
into that house ever again.

IRINA All right. That's all right. We'll all just sit here for
a while and not speak at all.

KULYGIN I took this beard and moustache from a boy in the
third form yesterday. *(He puts it on.)* Look, Masha.
Look. Who's this? Who am I?

OLGA Who?

KULYGIN Our German master! *(Laughs)* Isn't this exactly
what he's like, Masha?

MASHA Yes.

KULYGIN There!

OLGA Very like him.

KULYGIN Like him? It's him! *(In heavy German accent)* 'I
look and I say to me: who is beautiful three sisters
what sits in those garden—ja?'

> IRINA *laughs. Then* OLGA. *Finally* MASHA. *The
> laughter lives for a few seconds and then dies. Now*
> MASHA *cries again, quietly and in resignation.*
> NATASHA *enters, talking to the maid who trots
> behind her.*

NATASHA Two things I want done: bring Master Bobik up-
stairs and wash his hands and face—*(the maid is
about to leave:* NATASHA *shouts at her)*—I said two
things, didn't I? Are you thick? *(Controlled again)*
He's inside playing with Mister Protopopov. And
tell Mister Prozorov to take Miss Sophie for a walk

along the bank of the river. *(The maid exits. To the sisters)* Children! Never a moment to call your own. You girls don't know how lucky you are. *(To* IRINA*)* And you're leaving us tomorrow, Irina. That's a shame. Could you not stay on for another week? *(Now seeing* KULYGIN *for the first time.)* Jesus, Mary and Joseph! You put the heart across me!

KULYGIN *(German accent)* What means I put the heart across you?

He removes the mask.

NATASHA You're a bold, bold boy, Fyodor—that's what you are. Isn't he? *(To* IRINA*)* I've got so used to having you in the house that I'm going to miss you terribly. I really am. Yes, that's just what I'll do— Andrey can move into your room and he can saw away on his fiddle to his heart's content back there and he'll bother nobody. And wee Sophie, she can move into his room. That's that all sorted now. She's a real darling, isn't she? If you'd seen her this morning when she woke up. D'you know what she did? She smiled up at me—this is as true as God— and she said, 'Mama'. It was very . . . aesthetic.

KULYGIN There's no doubt about it—she's a very pretty child.

NATASHA So from tomorrow I'm to be all alone here then? Well—c'est la vie. The first thing I'll do is get that avenue of fir-trees cut down and then get rid of that maple—it's such a depressing aul' thing in the dark evenings. *(To* IRINA*)* And you're wearing a green sash, darling. Imagine. I wouldn't have thought green was your colour. But against the white I suppose it is quite . . . distinctive. And I'm going to plant flowers everywhere—all kinds of flowers—all over the place. I want the whole garden to be saturated with aromic . . . aromas. *(The maid has entered again—just as* NATASHA *discovers a fork lying on the ground.)* What's that fork doing here? *(In a fury)* What in God's name is a valuable, stamped-silver fork lying out here for? And don't you dare answer me back, madam—don't you dare!

She pursues the maid off.

KULYGIN   There she goes again.

A military band plays in the distance.

OLGA   Listen. They're leaving.

They all listen. CHEBUTYKIN *enters.*

MASHA   God be with him. God be with them all . . .
(Suddenly brisk, to KULYGIN*)* We'd better go home.
Where's my hat and coat?
KULYGIN   I left them inside. I'll get them.

He exits.

OLGA   Yes; it's time we all went home.

CHEBUTYKIN   *(Softly)* Olga.

*She looks at him. He beckons to her. She goes to
him.*

OLGA   What is it?
CHEBUTYKIN   Nothing . . . I don't know how to say it . . .

He whispers in her ear.

OLGA   Oh my God!
CHEBUTYKIN   I know . . . shocking . . . what's there to say . . .
I feel ancient.
MASHA   What's wrong, Olga?

OLGA *goes to* IRINA *and puts her arms around her.*

OLGA   My darling—my darling—there's been a terrible
accident. I don't know how to ——
IRINA   What is it? Tell me quickly—what is it? *(Momentary
pause.)* For God's sake *tell* me, Olga.
OLGA   The baron has been killed in a duel.

IRINA *stares at her, then at* CHEBUTYKIN, *then back*

at OLGA. *A long pause. Then she begins to cry quietly.*

IRINA   I knew it . . . I knew it . . .

CHEBUTYKIN *goes to the back of the stage and sits.*

CHEBUTYKIN   Ancient and exhausted . . .

He takes out a paper, looks at it, lets it fall to the ground.

CHEBUTYKIN   Crying's no harm . . . they say that a good cry can even be salutary, if being salutary matters . . . *(Sings)* 'When I found she'd left me in the lurch, Oh how it did upset me . . .'

He cannot continue. He closes his eyes and slowly leans his head right back until it is resting on the back of the seat. The three sisters are close together.

MASHA   Listen to that music. They're going away forever. They'll never be back. And we must begin to put our lives together again because we have got to go on living. That's what we must do.

IRINA   *(Resting her head on Olga's shoulder)* All this unhappiness, all this suffering—what is it all for? Some day we'll understand. Some day we'll know the answer. But in the meantime life must go on and we must work and work and think of nothing but work. I'll go off by myself tomorrow and teach in a school somewhere and spend the rest of my life serving people who need me. It's autumn now. It will be winter soon, and the snow will come and cover everything everywhere, and I will keep on working and working.

OLGA *puts her arms around* MASHA *and* IRINA.

OLGA   Just listen to that music. It's so assured, so courageous. It makes you want to go on, doesn't it? Oh my God! Yes, of course we will die and be forgotten—

113

everything about us, how we looked, how we spoke, that there were three of us. But our unhappiness, our suffering, won't be wasted. They're a preliminary to better times, and because of them the people who come after us will inherit a better life—a life of peace and content and happiness. And they will look on us with gratitude and with love. But our life isn't over yet. By no means! We are going to go on living! And that music is so confident, so courageous, it almost seems as if it is about to be revealed very soon why we are alive and what our suffering is for. If only we knew that. If only we knew that.

The music fades slowly. KULYGIN, *smiling bravely, enters with Masha's hat and coat and stands waiting with infinite patience.* ANDREY *enters at the back of the stage with his book and his pram and pauses.*

CHEBUTYKIN *(Sings softly)* 'There was I, waiting at the church,
Waiting at the church, waiting at the church;
When I found she'd left me in the lurch,
Oh how it did upset ——'

He stops abruptly, sits upright and stares in front of him.

CHEBUTYKIN Matters sweet damn all . . . sweet damn all it matters . . .
OLGA If we only knew. Oh, if we only knew.

BRING LIGHTS DOWN SLOWLY